# ESOS RELAJANTES DÍAS MUSICALES DE VERANO

# DEL LIBRO DE COLOREAR PARA ADULTOS

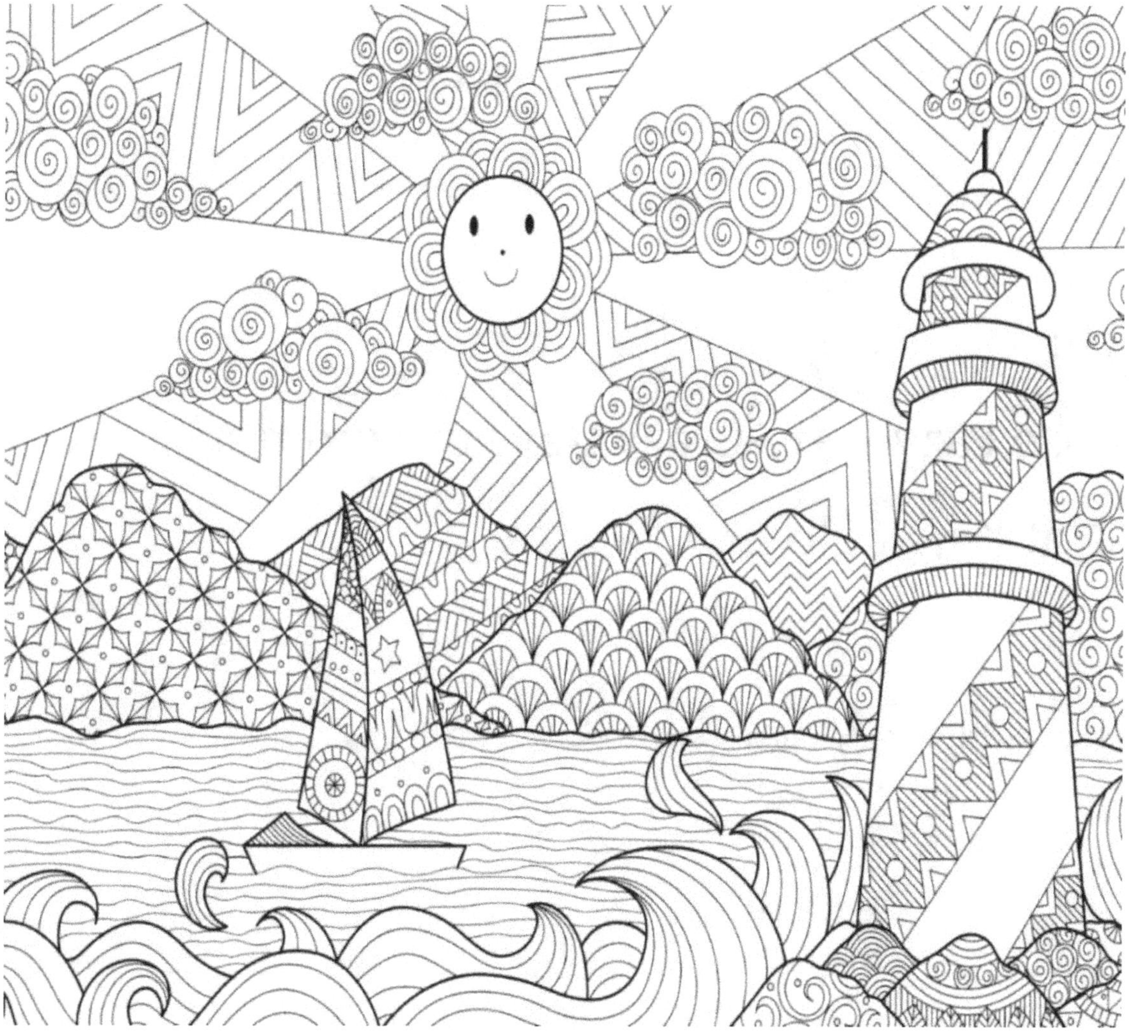

## By Gail Kamer

Toca:

"Those Lazy-Hazy-Crazy Days of Summer"

by Nat King Cole

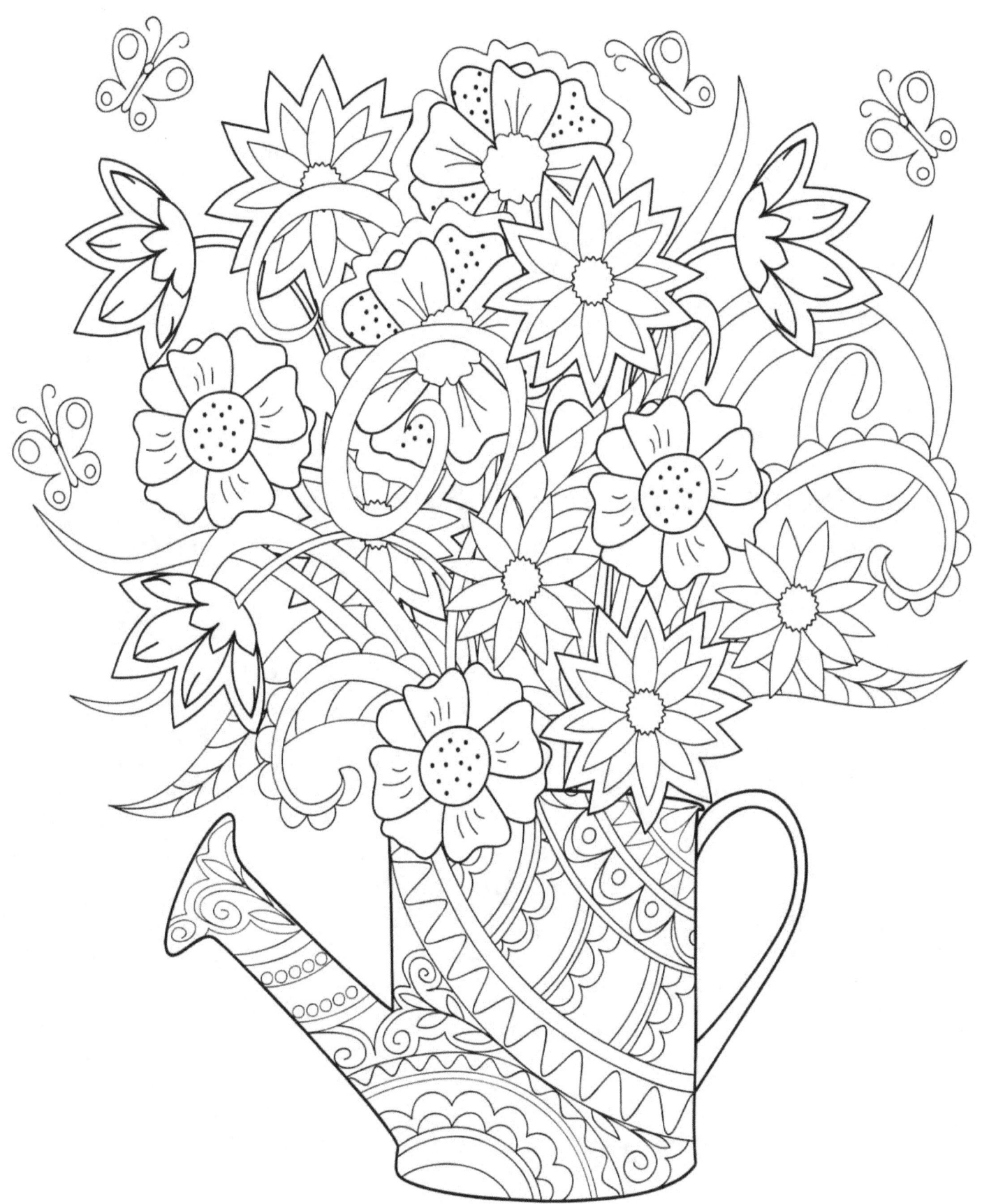

Toca: "Summertime" by Billy Stewart

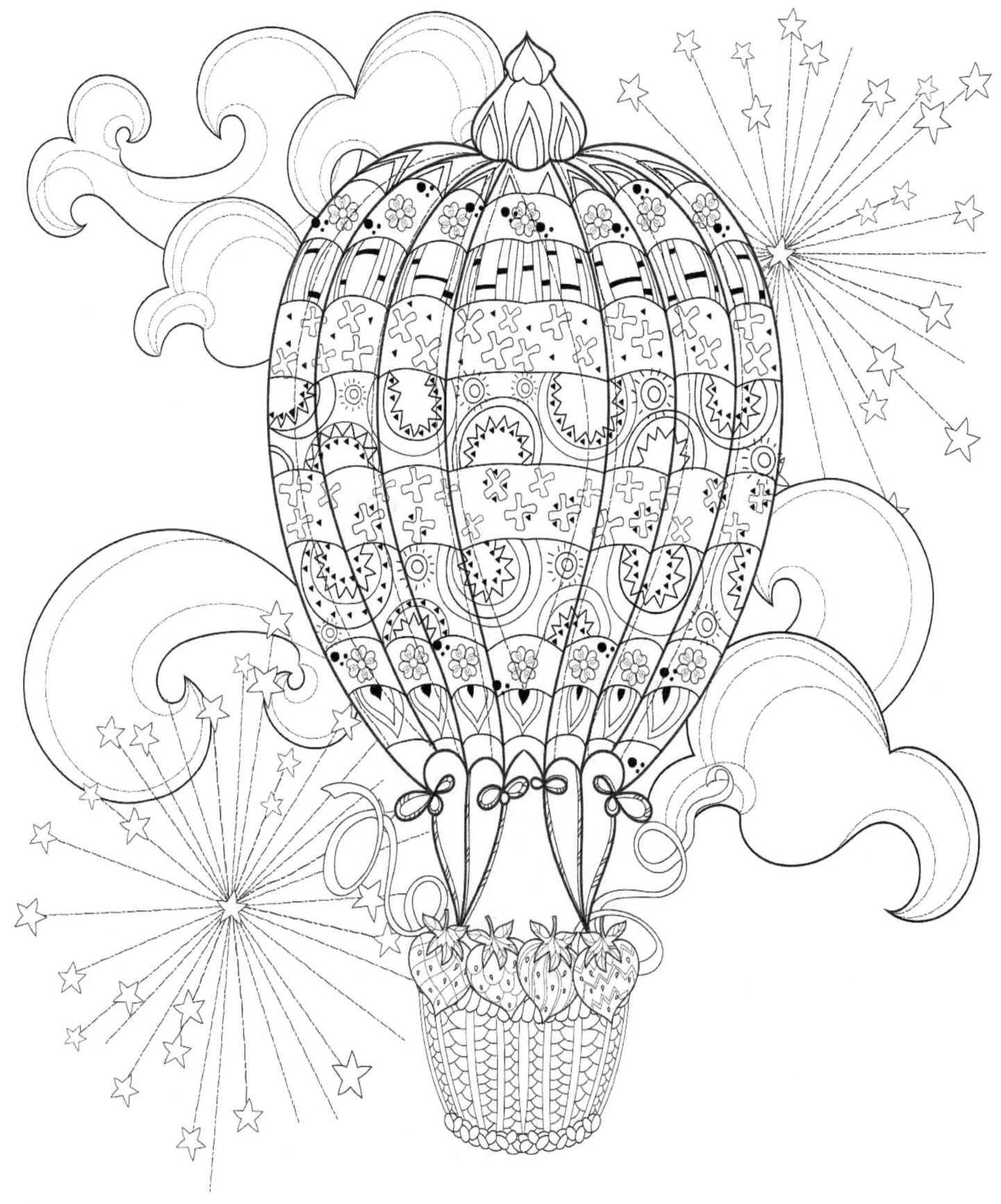

Toca:

"Summer Breeze" by Seals and Crofts

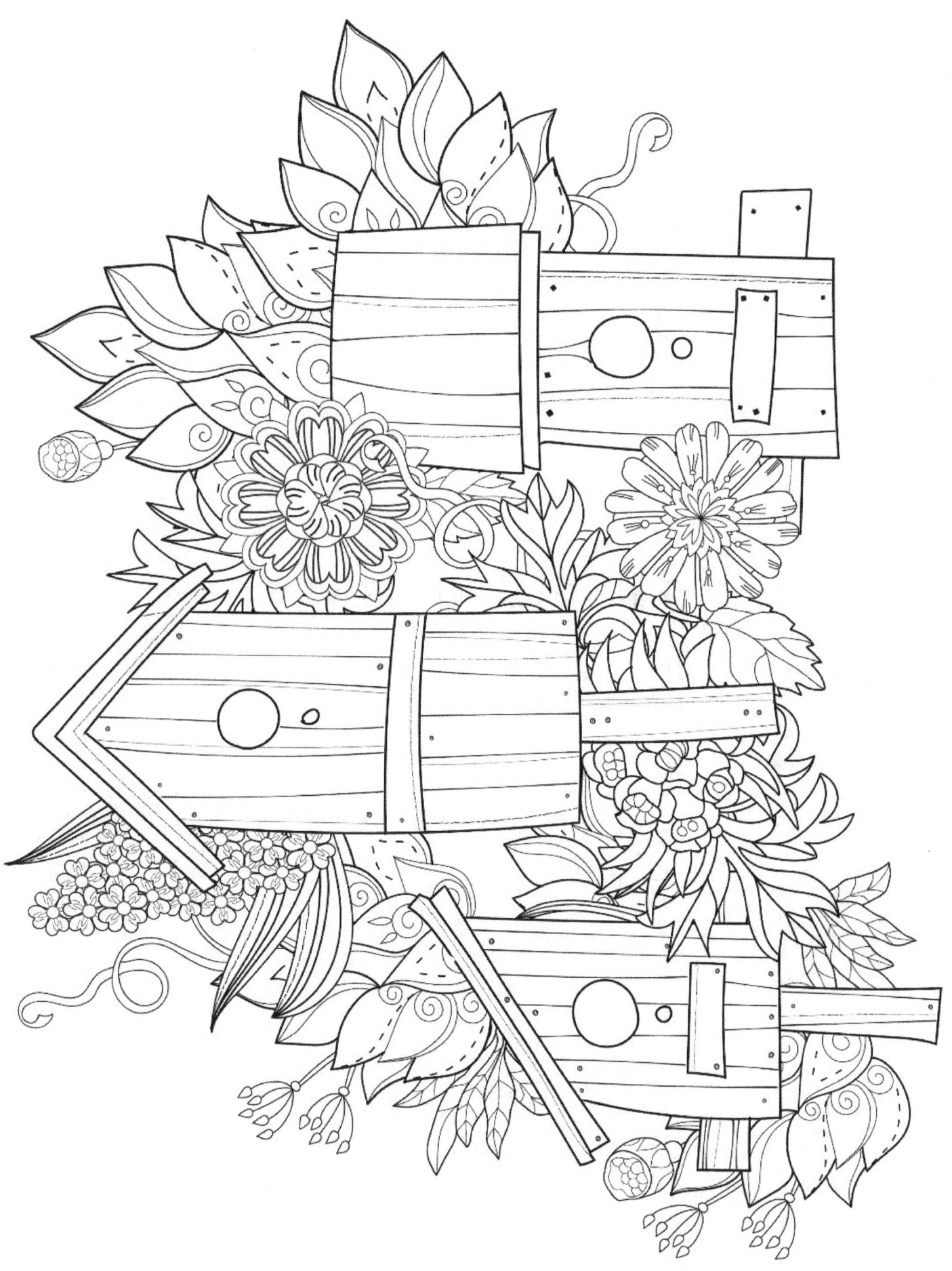

Toca: "Sittin' on the Dock of the Bay"

by Otis Redding

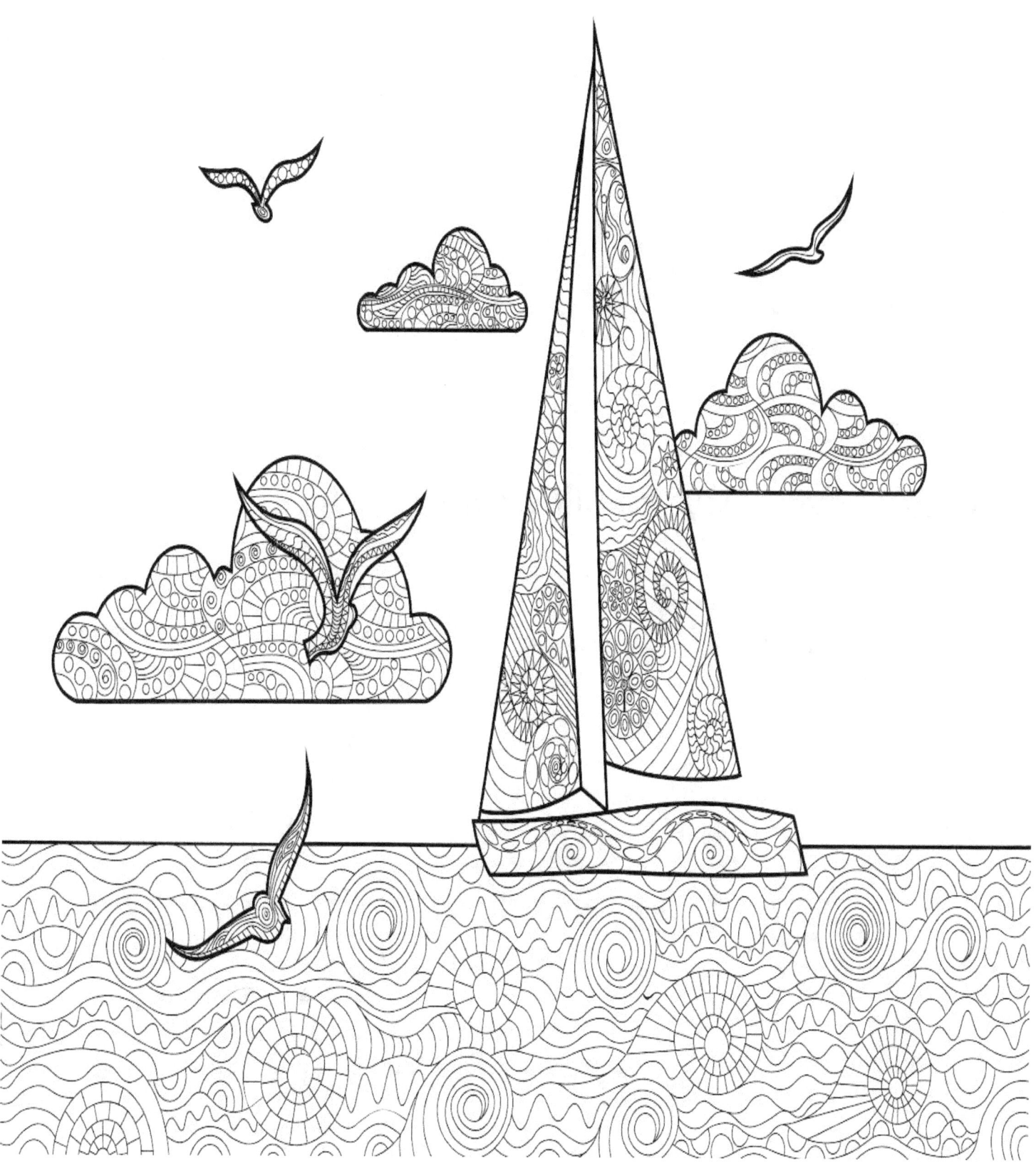

Toca: "Lovely Day" by Bill Withers

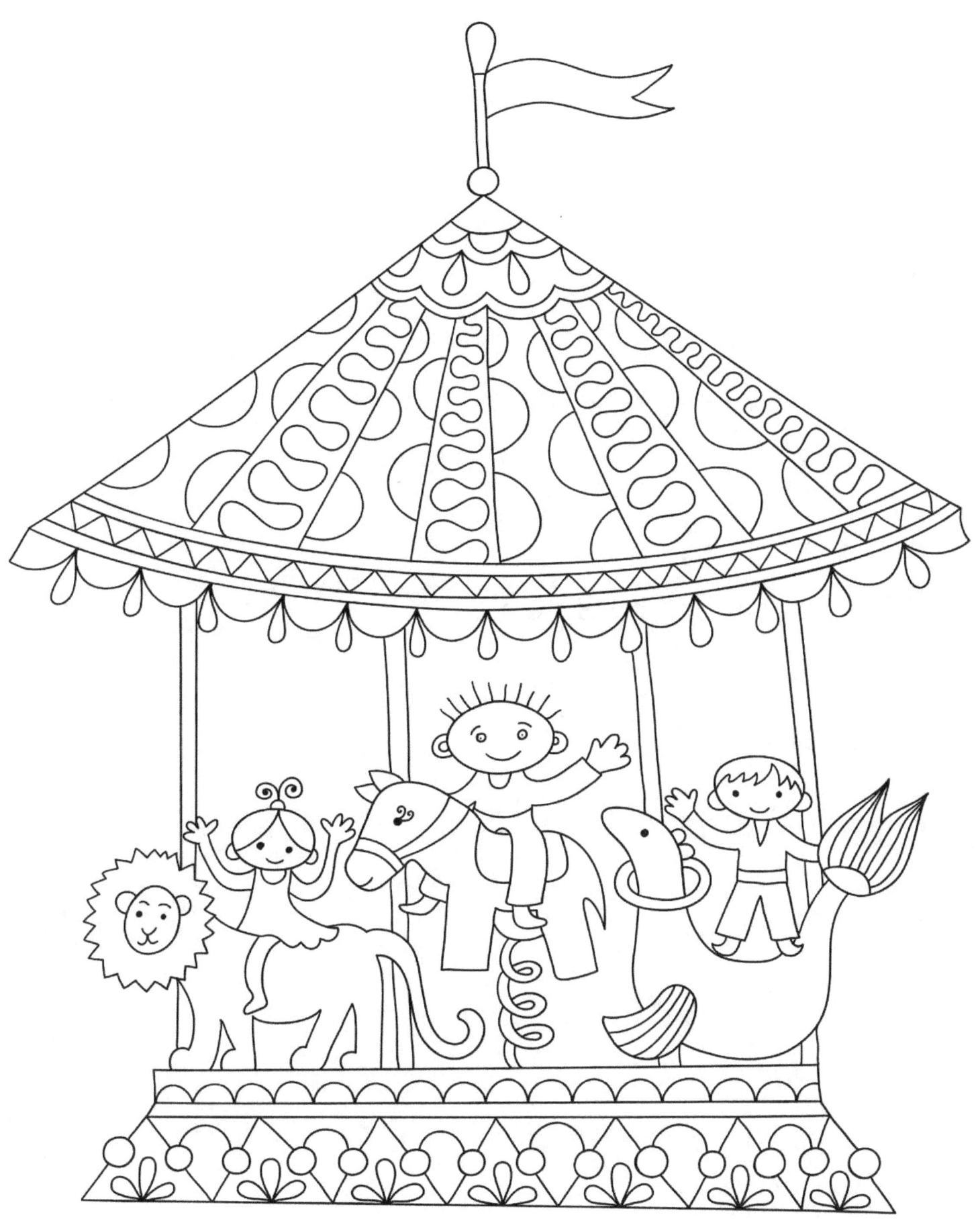

Toca: "Vacation" by Go Go's

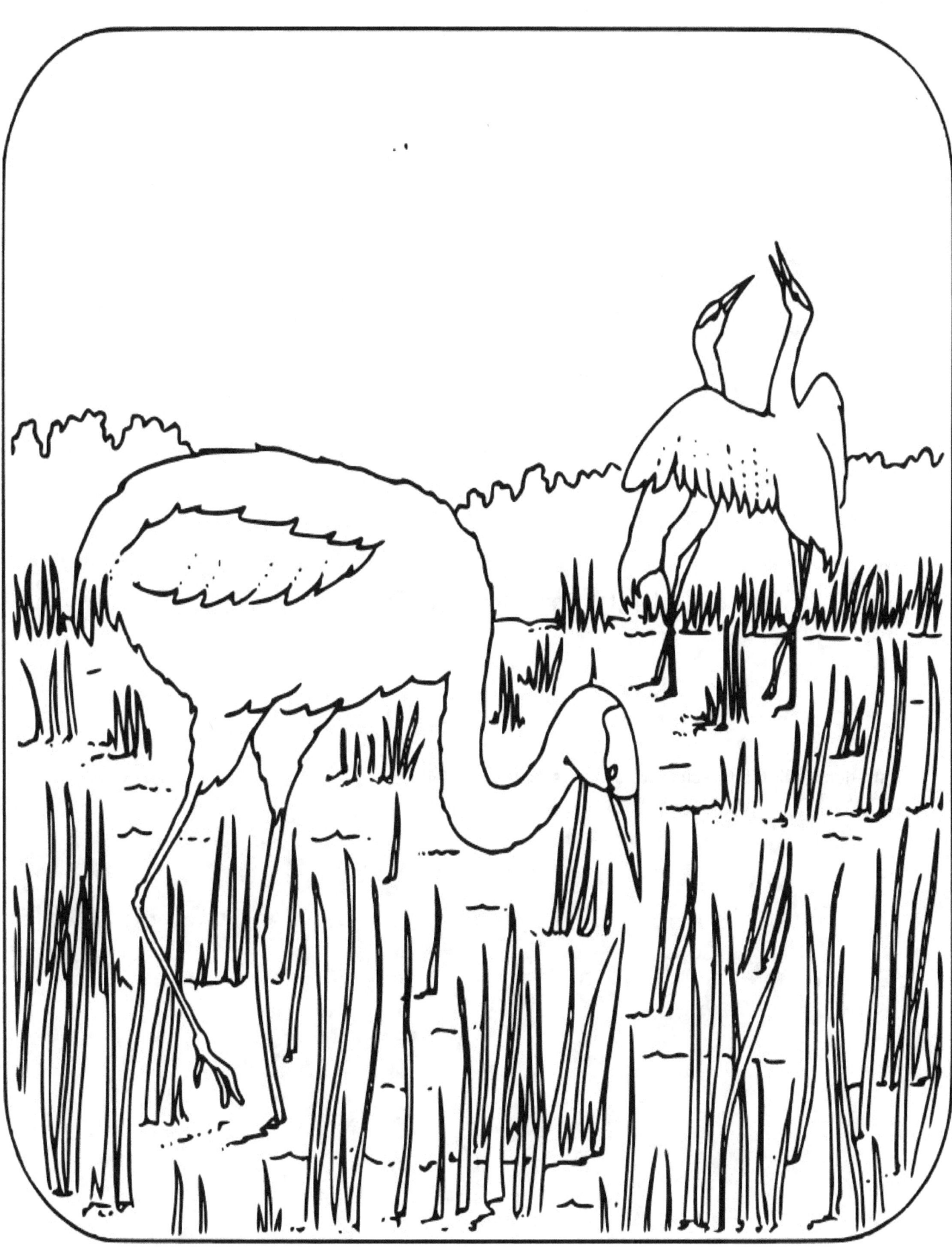

Toca: "Splish Splash" by Bobby Darin

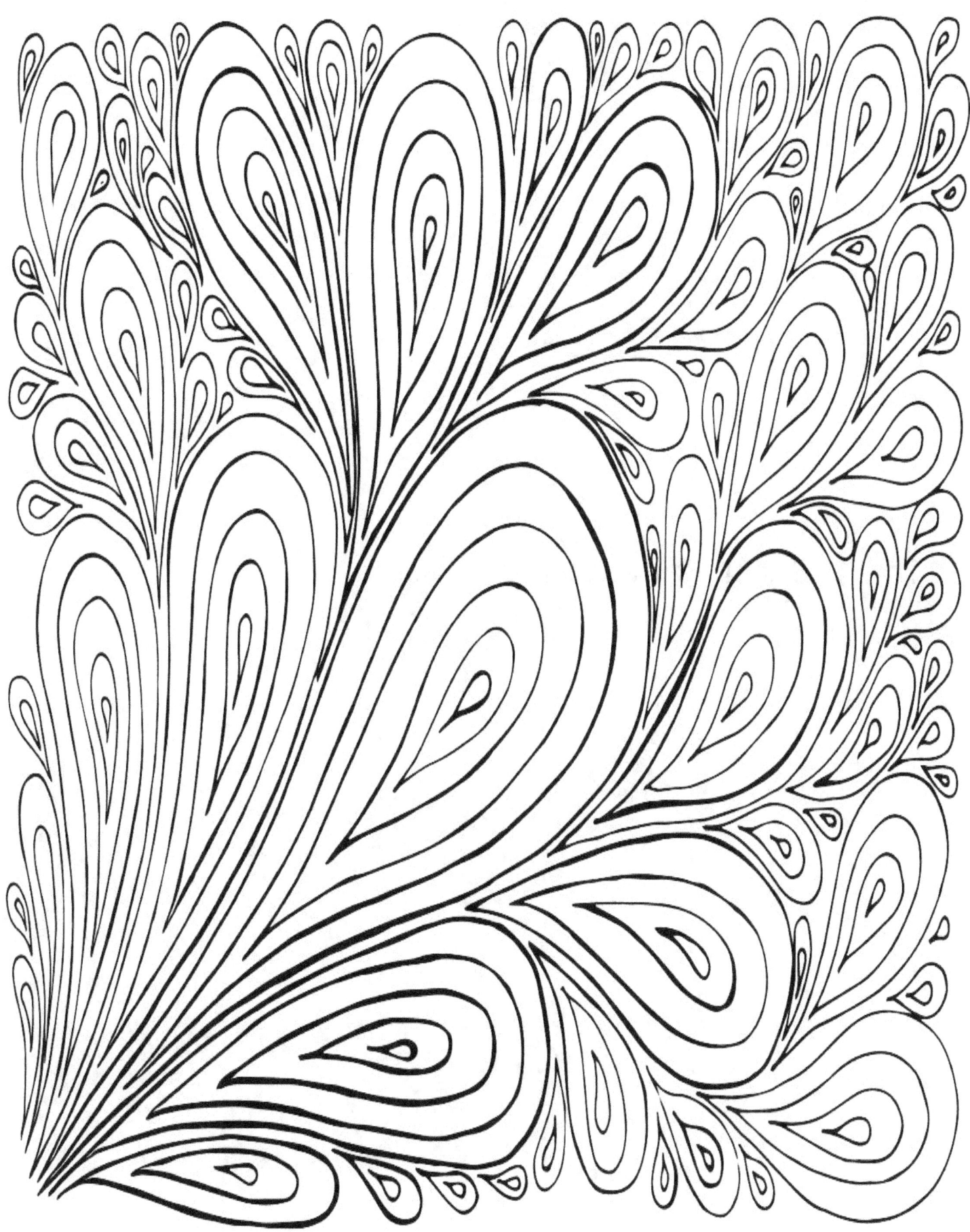

Toca: "Beach Baby" by First Class

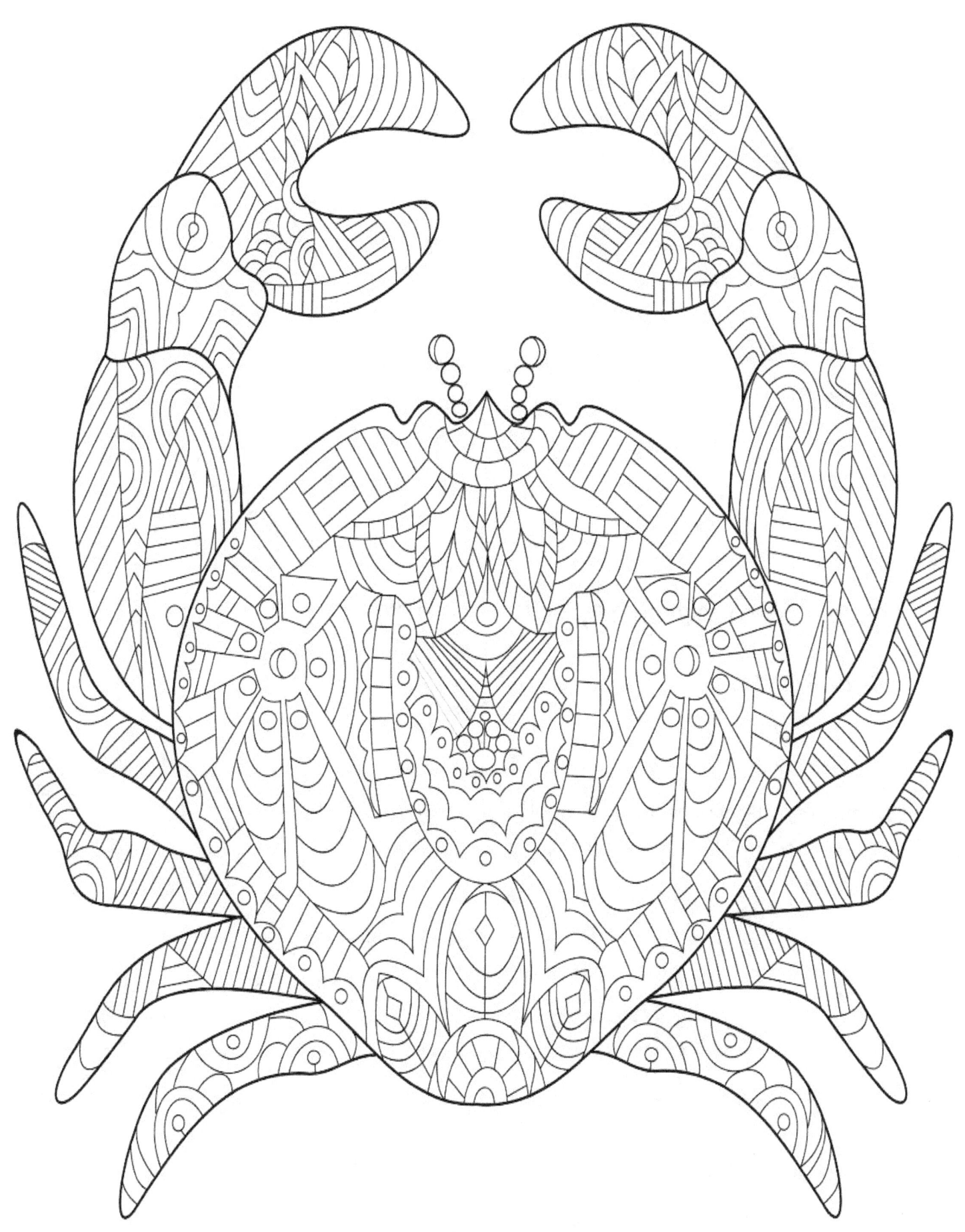

Toca: "Summertime, Summertime"

by Jamies

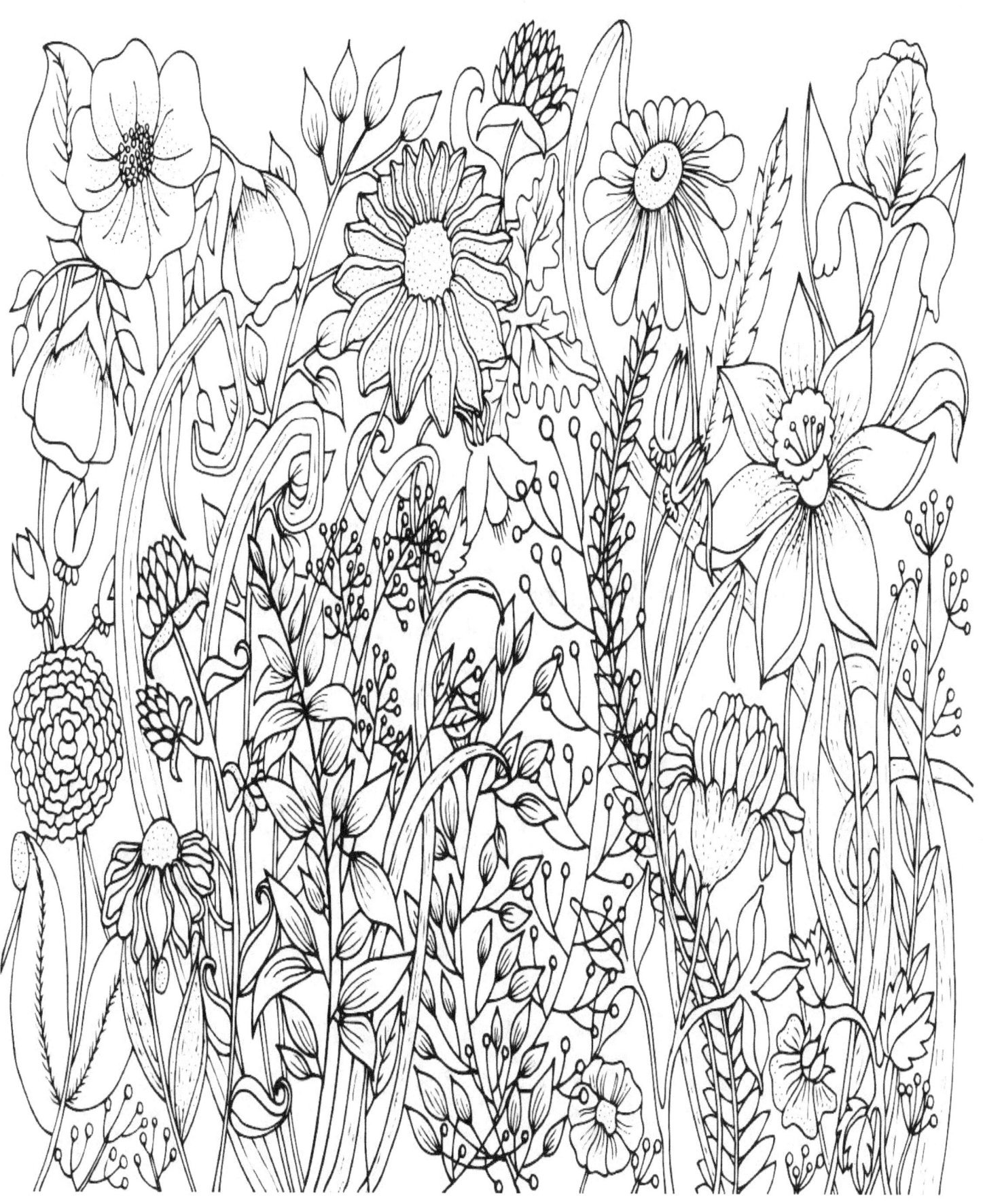

Toca:

"Boombastic/In the Summertime"

by Shaggy

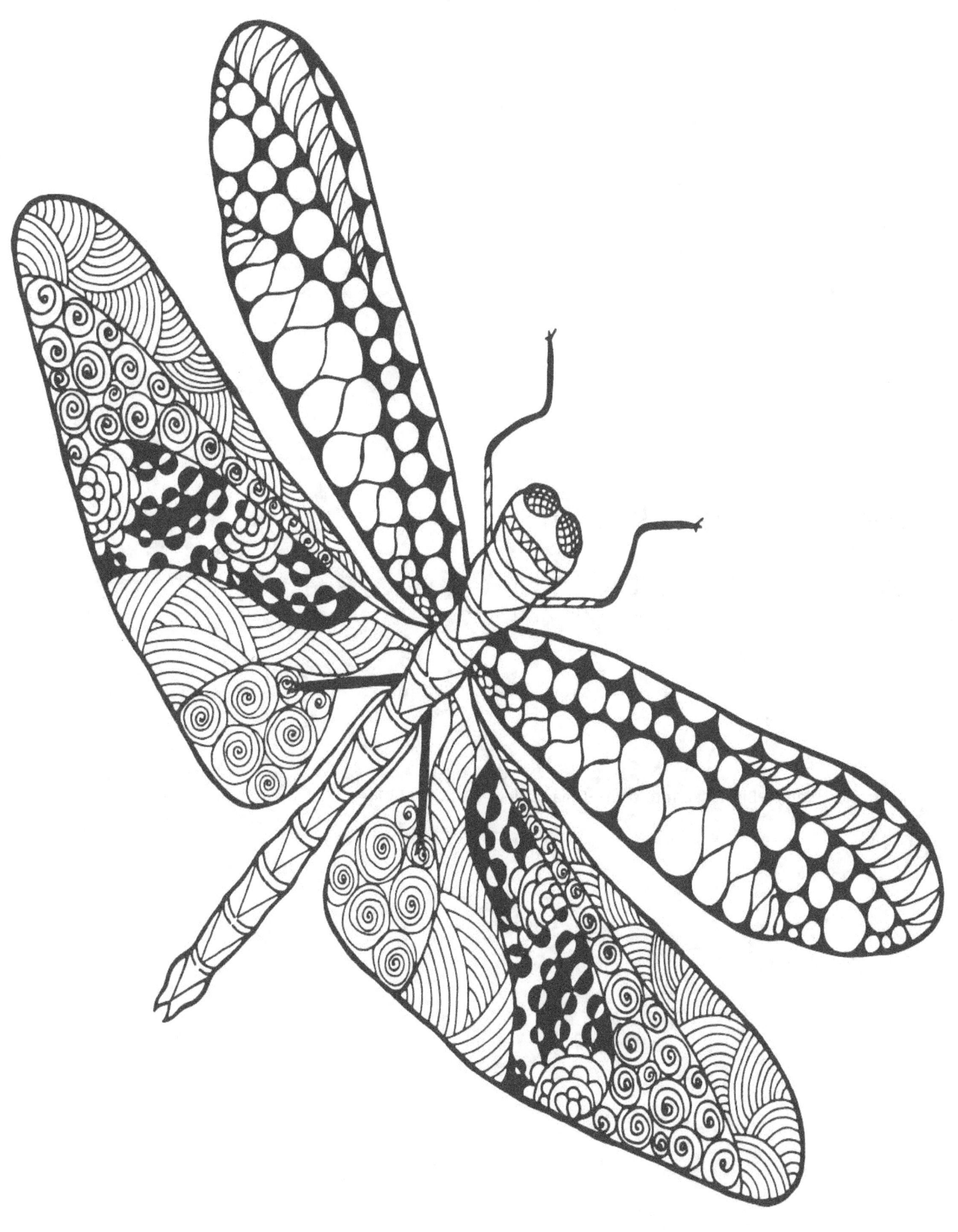

Toca: "Summer Breeze"

by Seals and Crofts

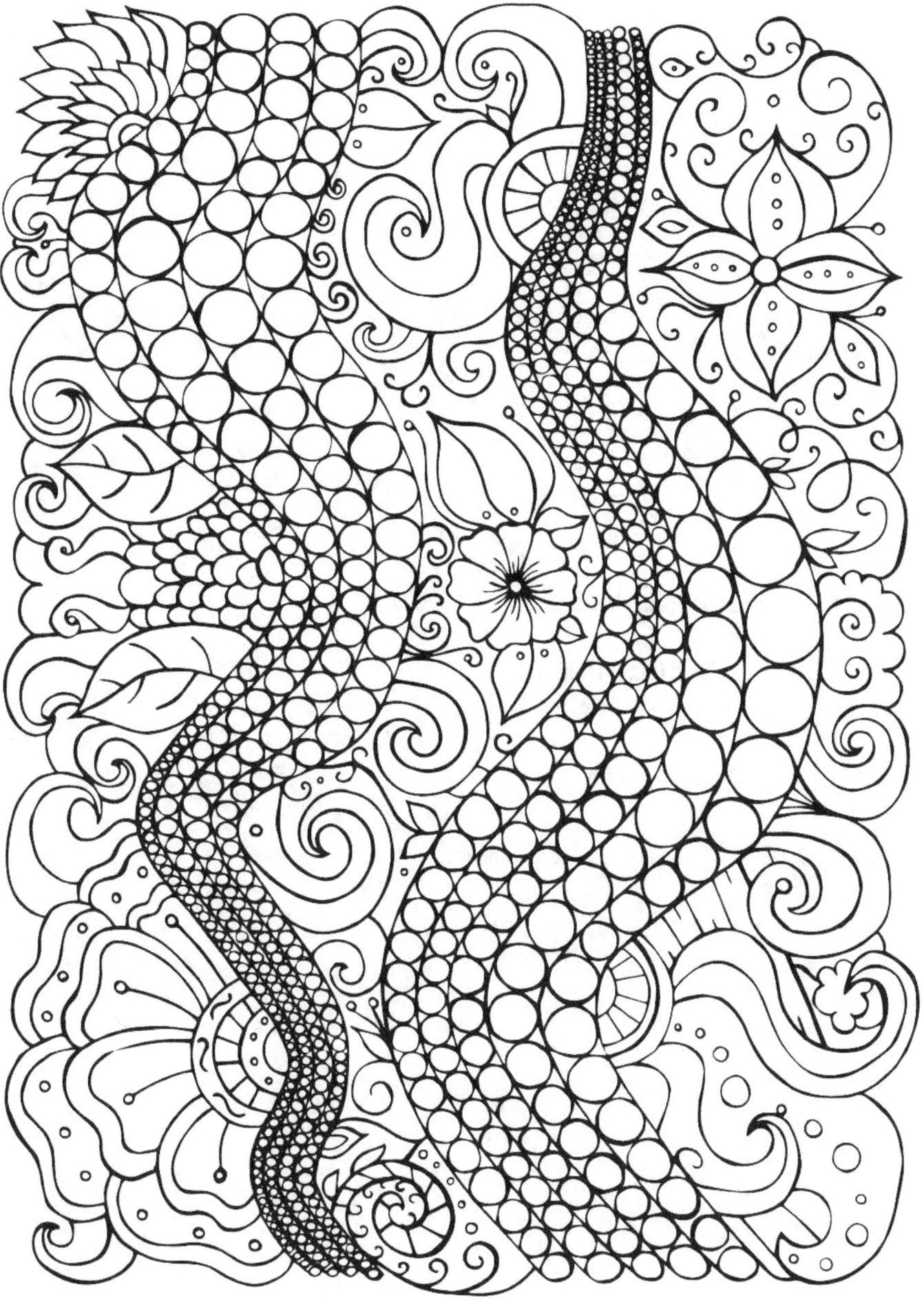

Toca: "Pocketful of Sunshine"

by Natasha Bedingfield

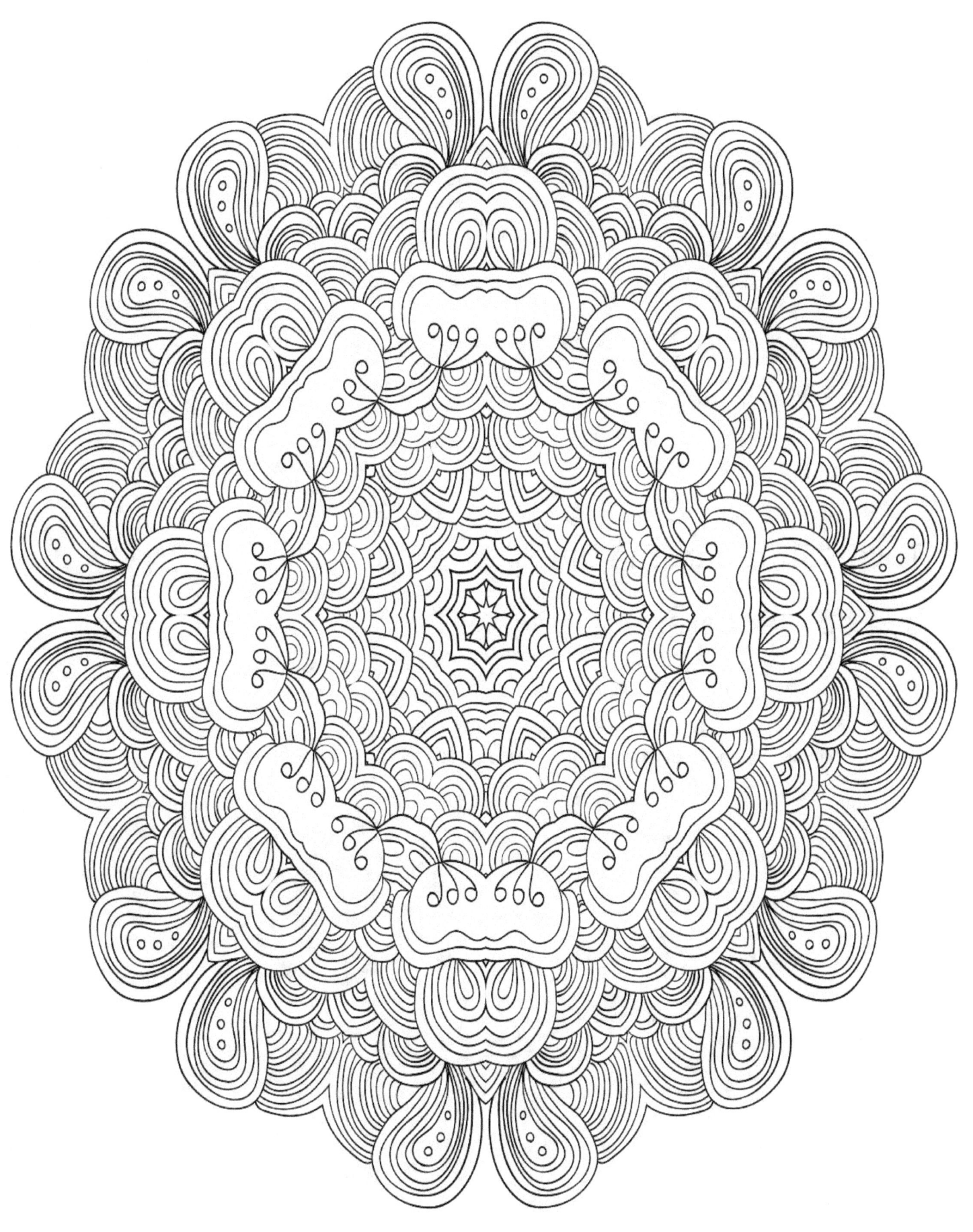

Toca: "Summertime Blues"

by Eddie Cochran

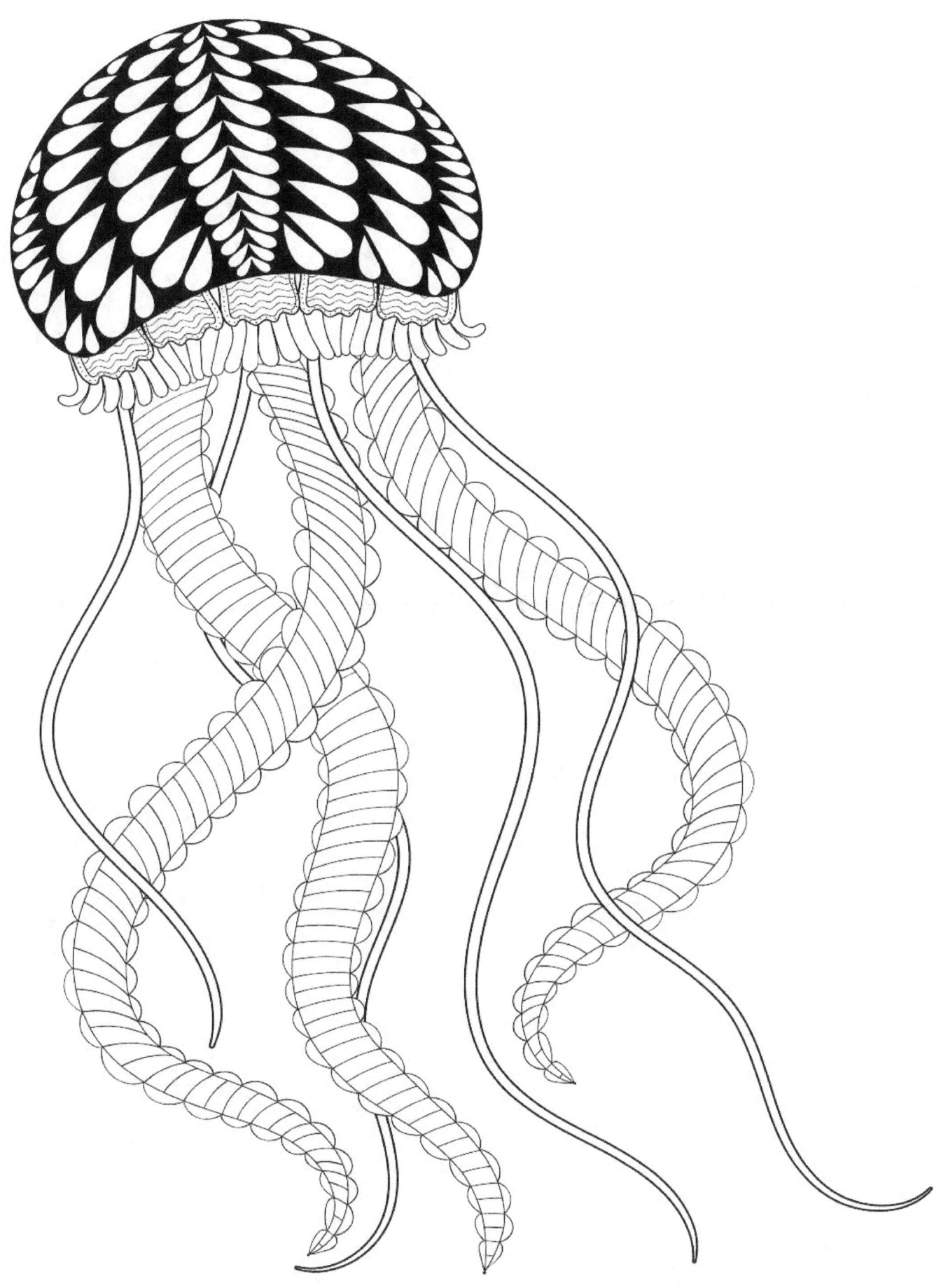

Toca: "Harbor Lights" by Bing Crosby

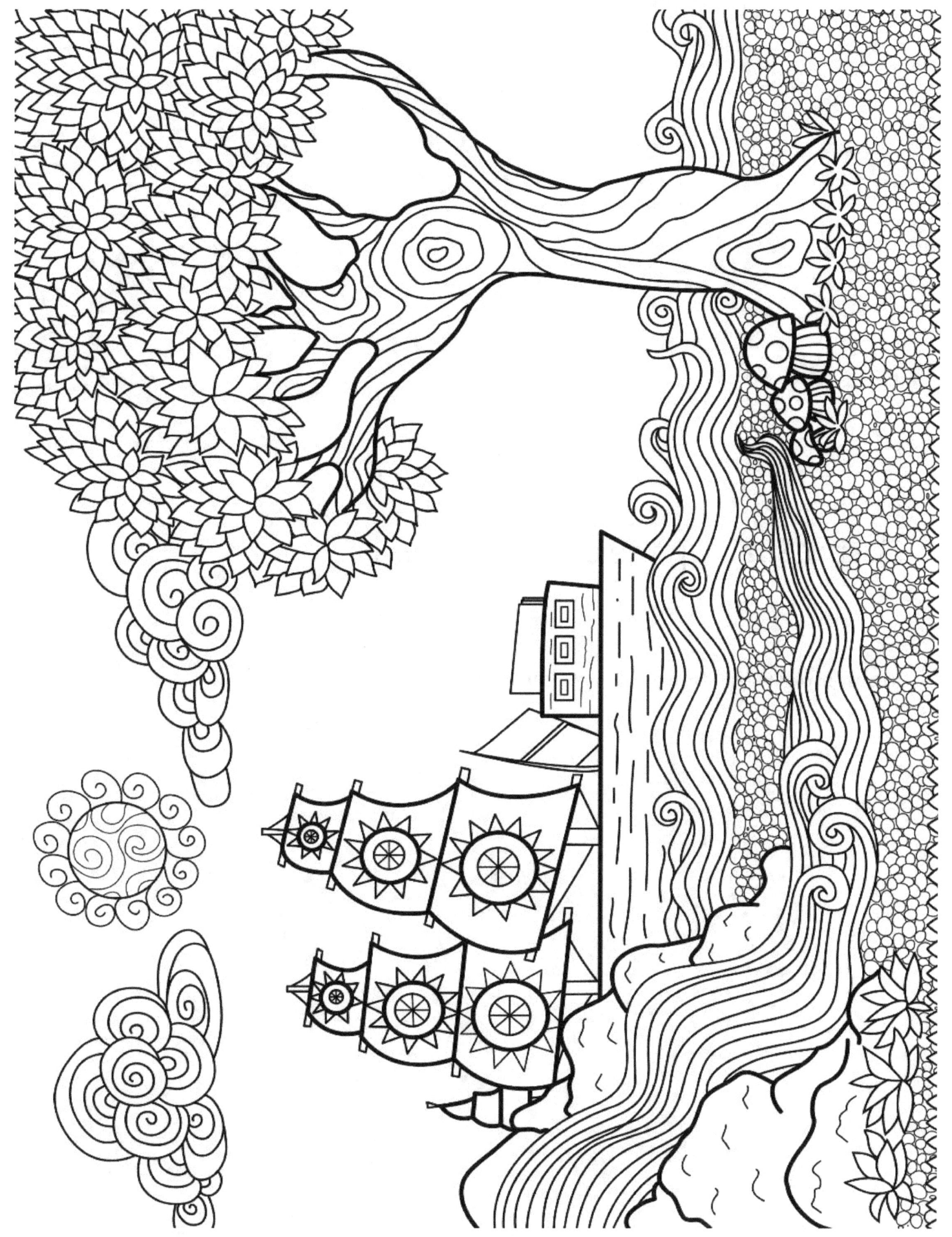

Toca: "Soak Up the Sun" by Cheryl Crow

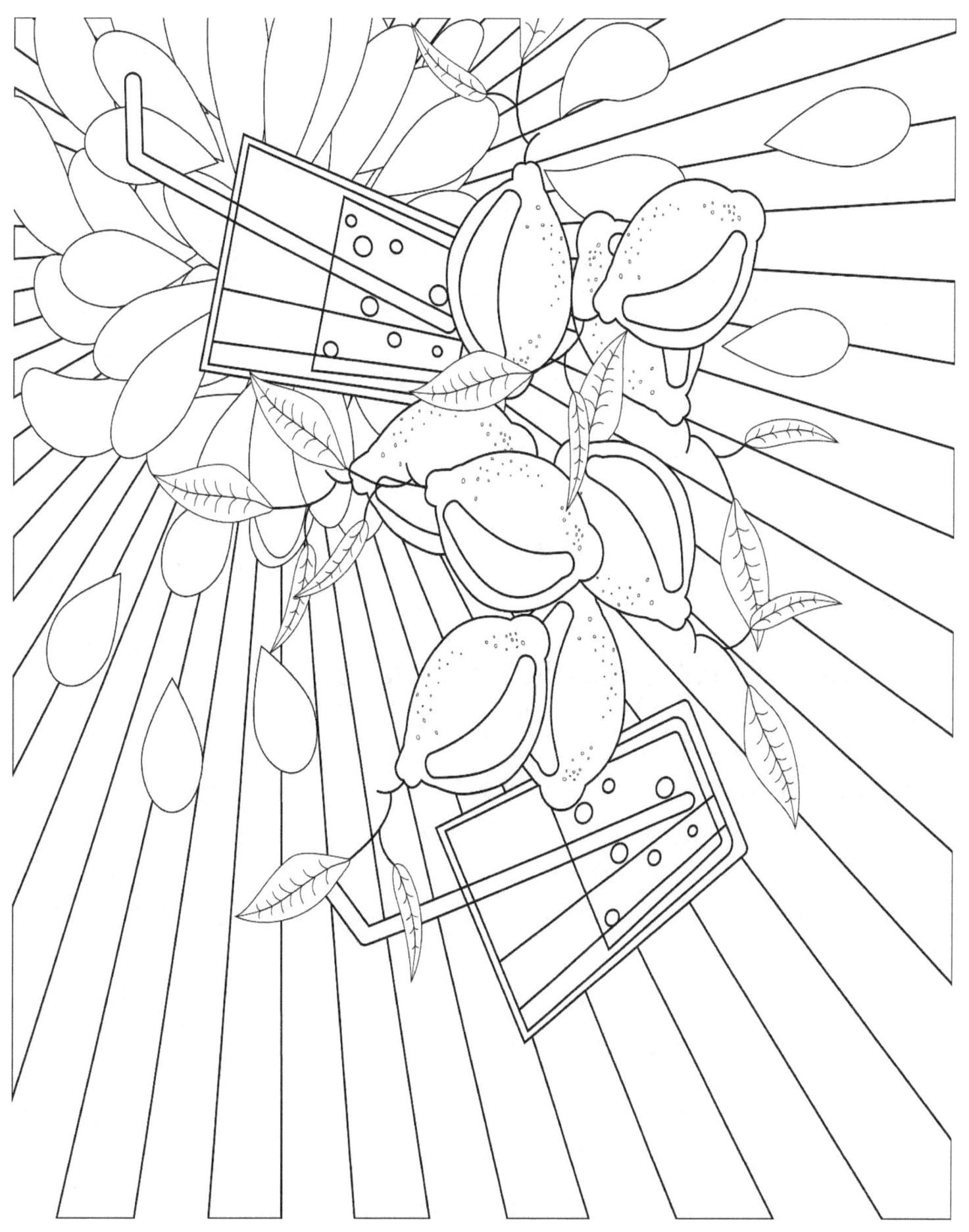

Toca:

"Summer Love" by Justin Timberlake

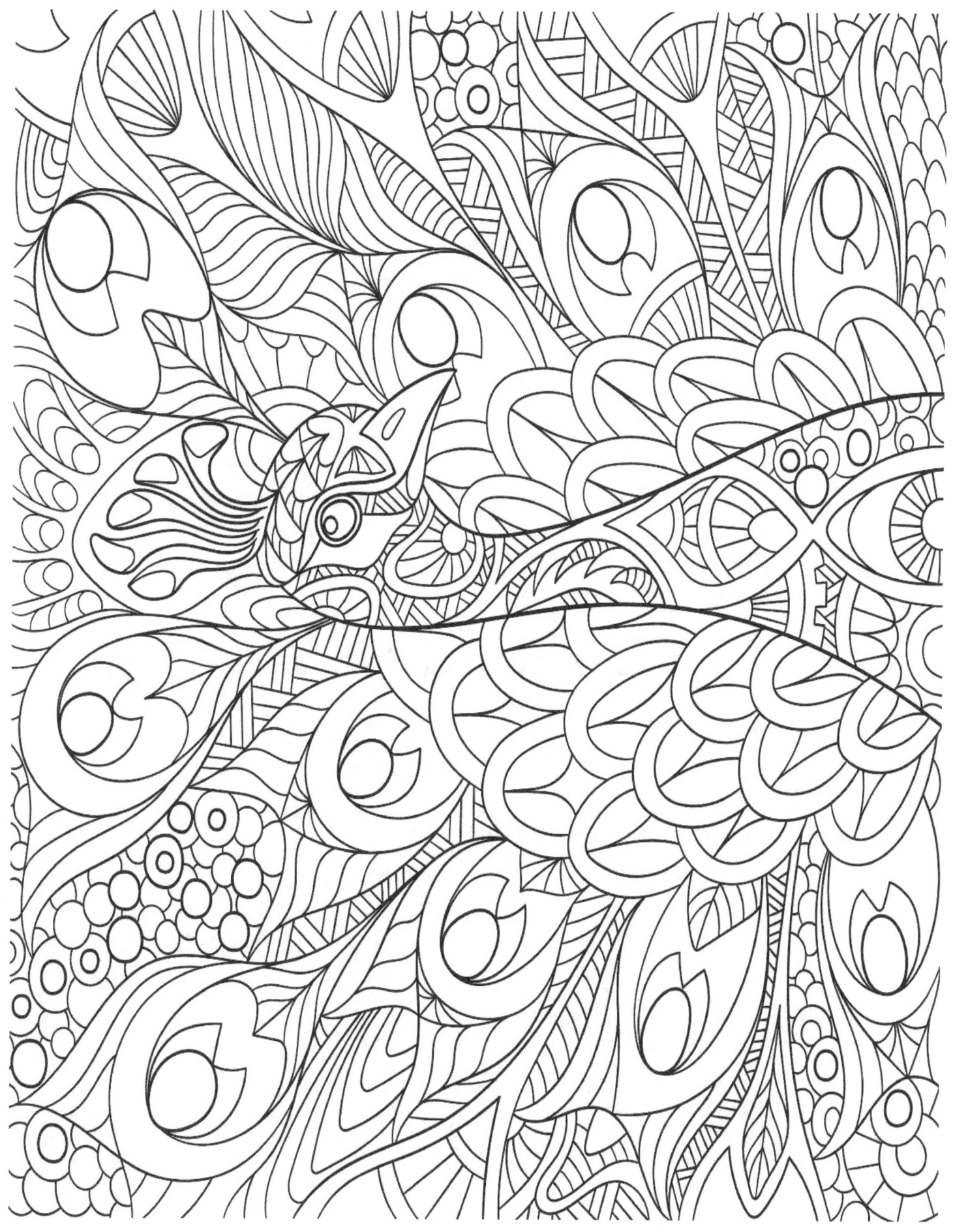

Toca: "Sweet Escape" by Gwen Stefani

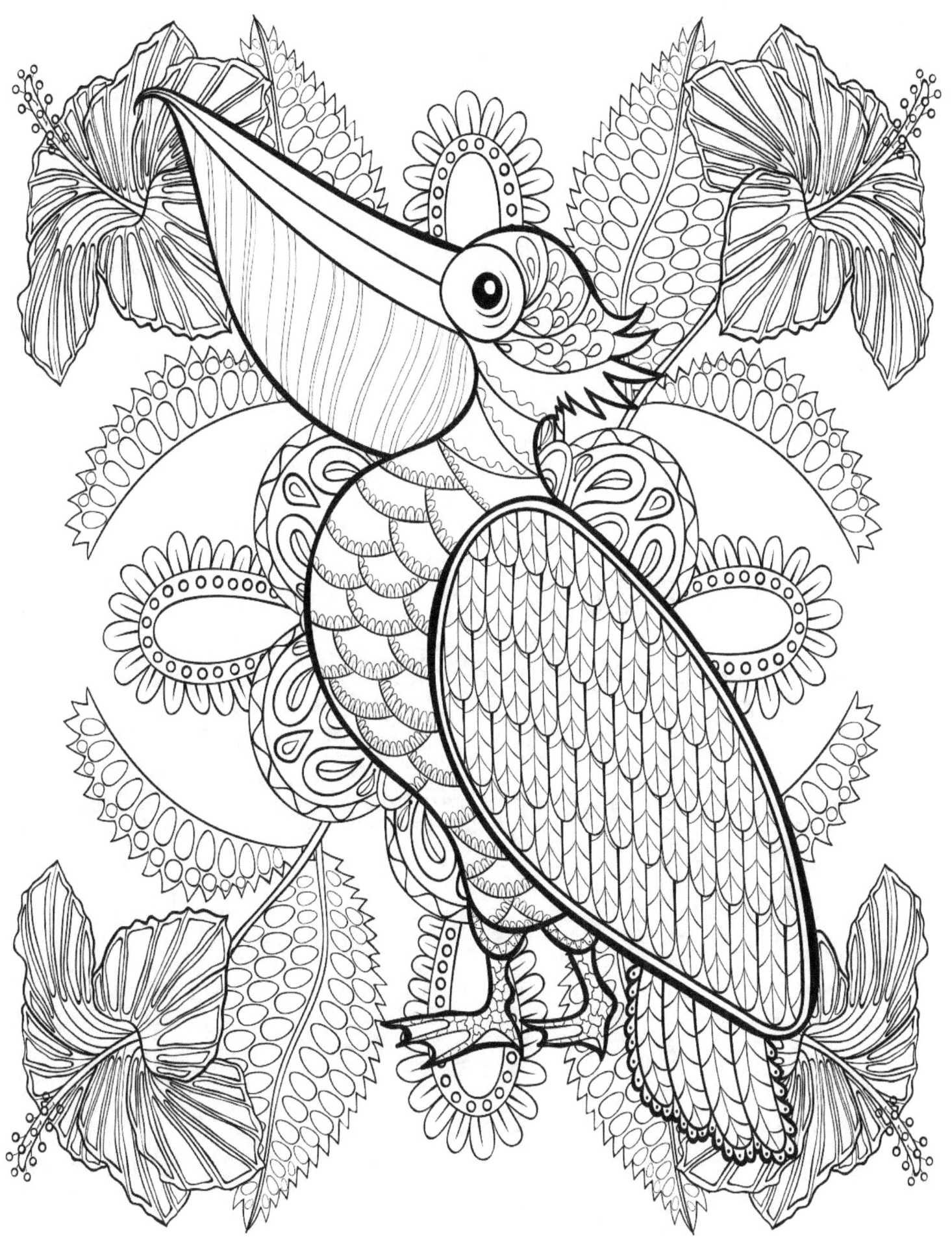

Toca: "Good Vibrations"

by Marky Mark and the Funky Bunch

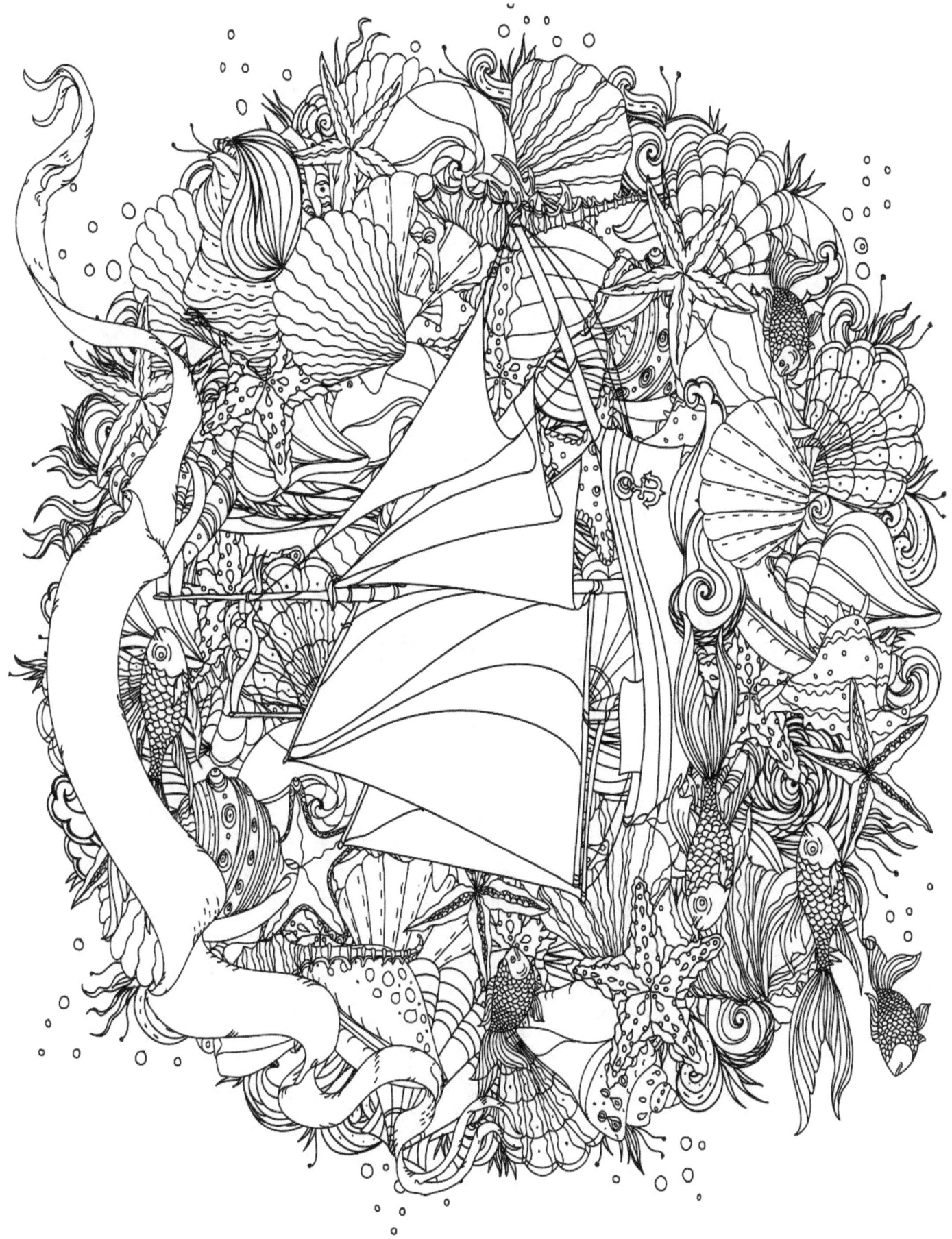

Toca: "Hot Fun in the Summertime"

by Sly and the Family Stone

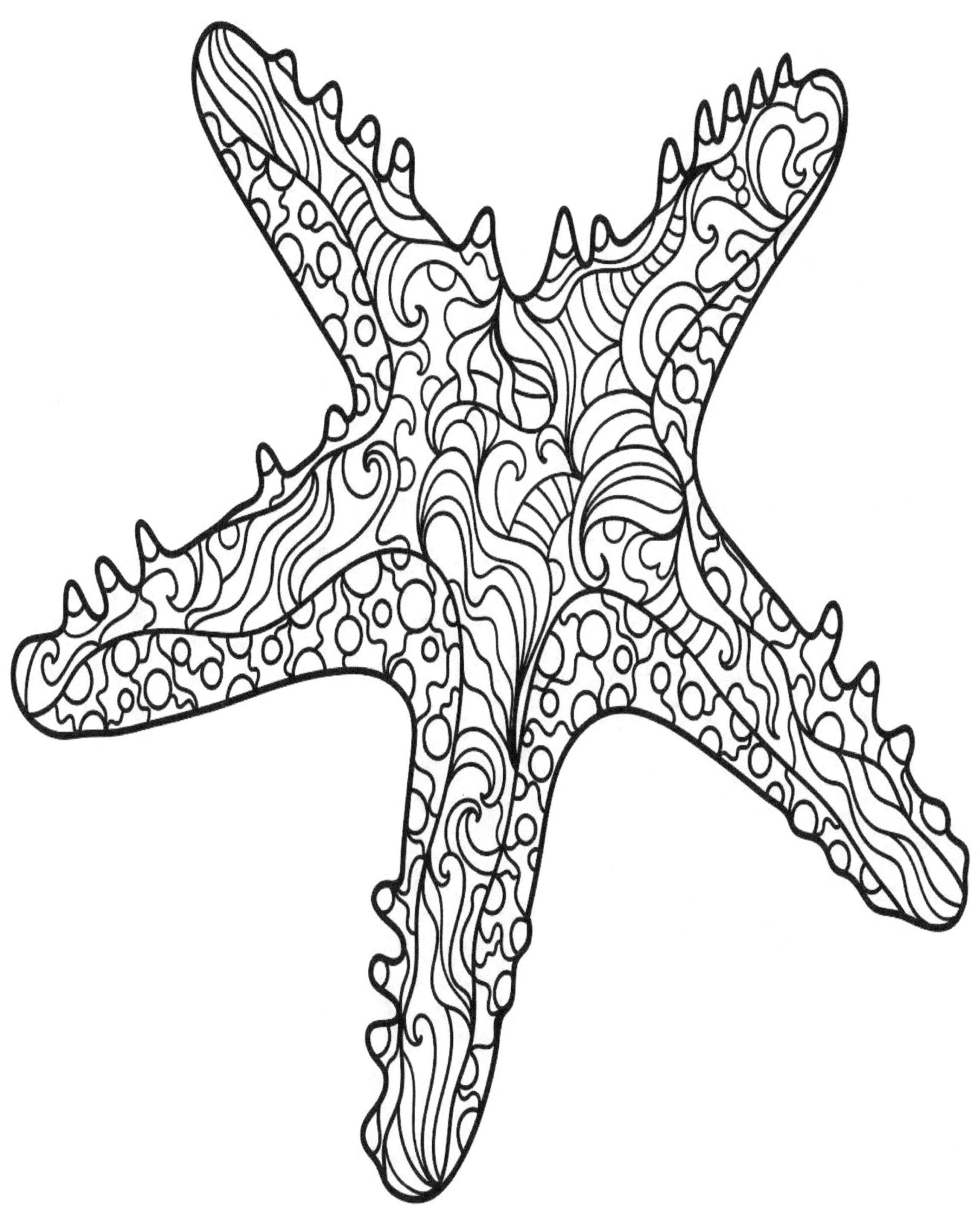

Toca: "All Summer Long" by Kid Rock

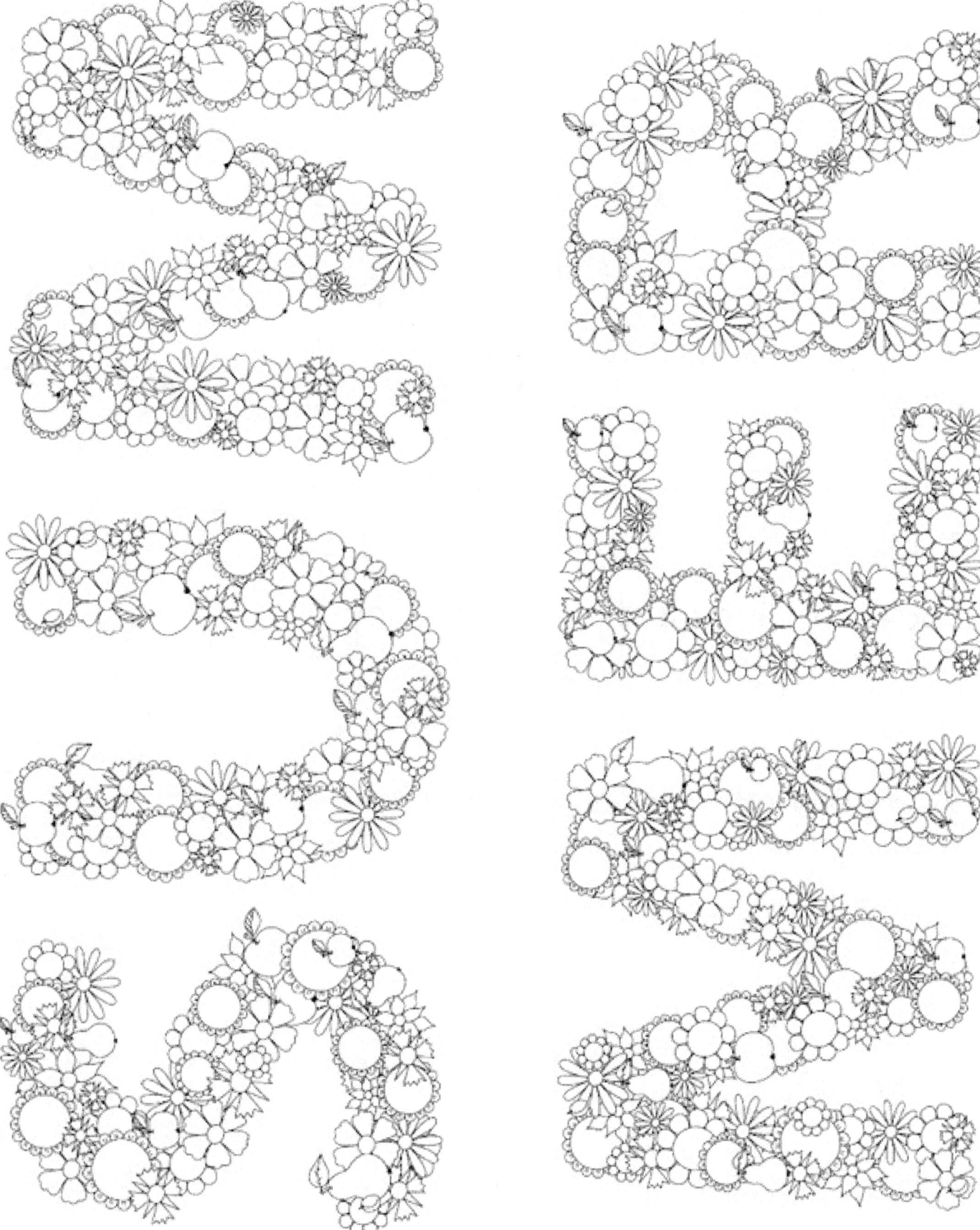

Toca:

"Beat This Summer" by Brad Paisley

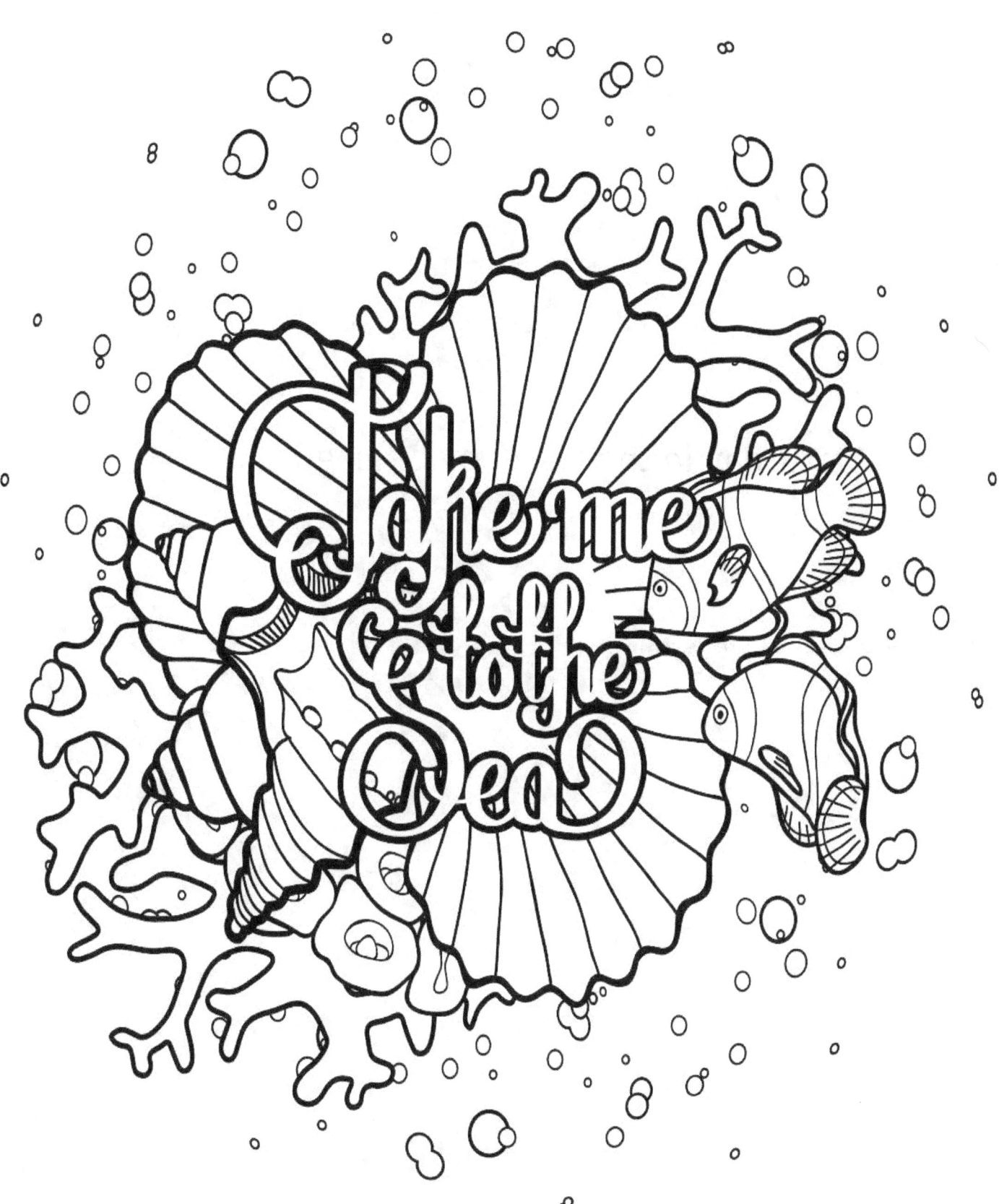

Toca: "Saturday in the Park" by Chicago

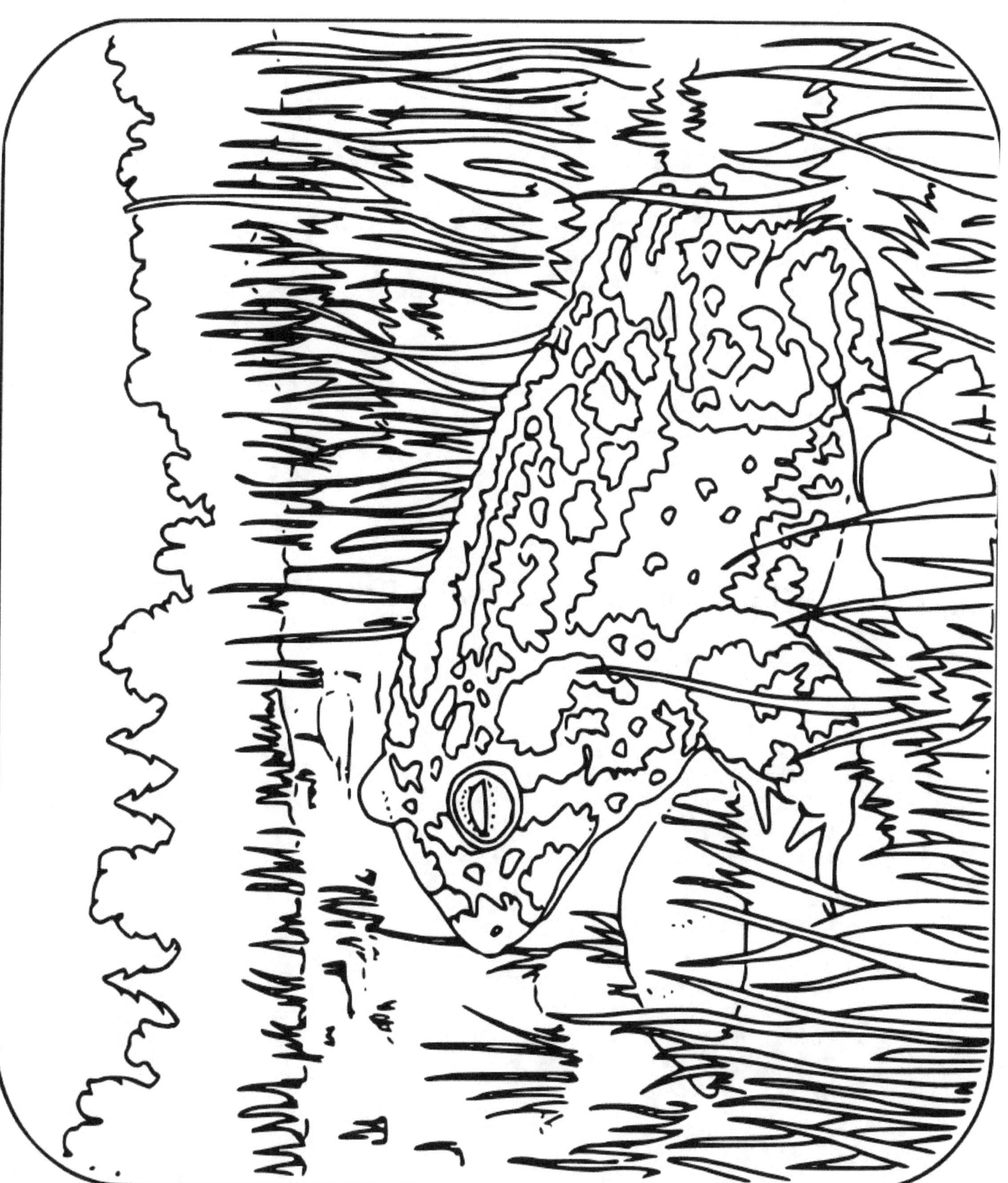

Toca: "Surfer Girls" by the Beach Boys

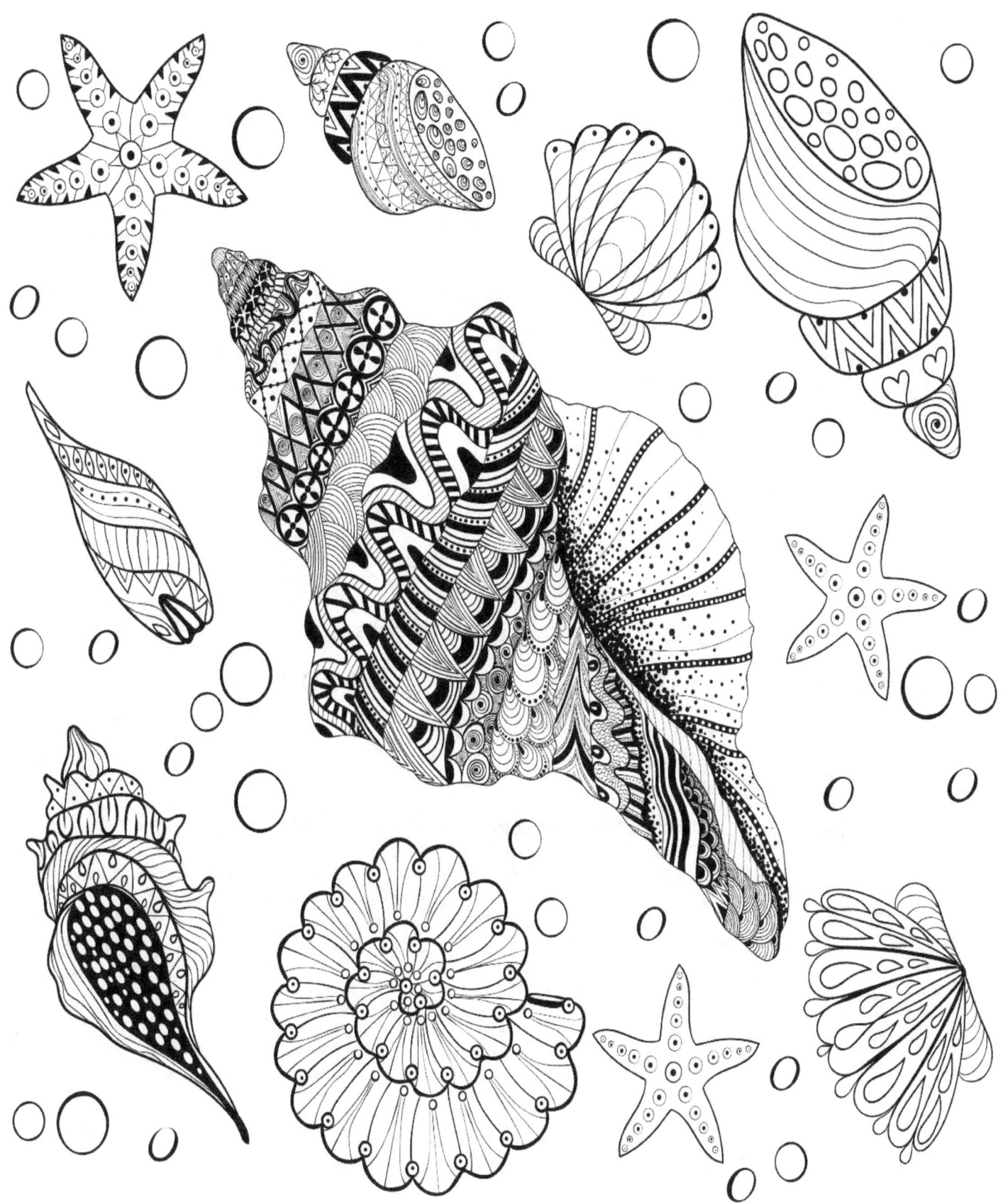

Toca:

"Love Letters in the Sand" by Pat Boone

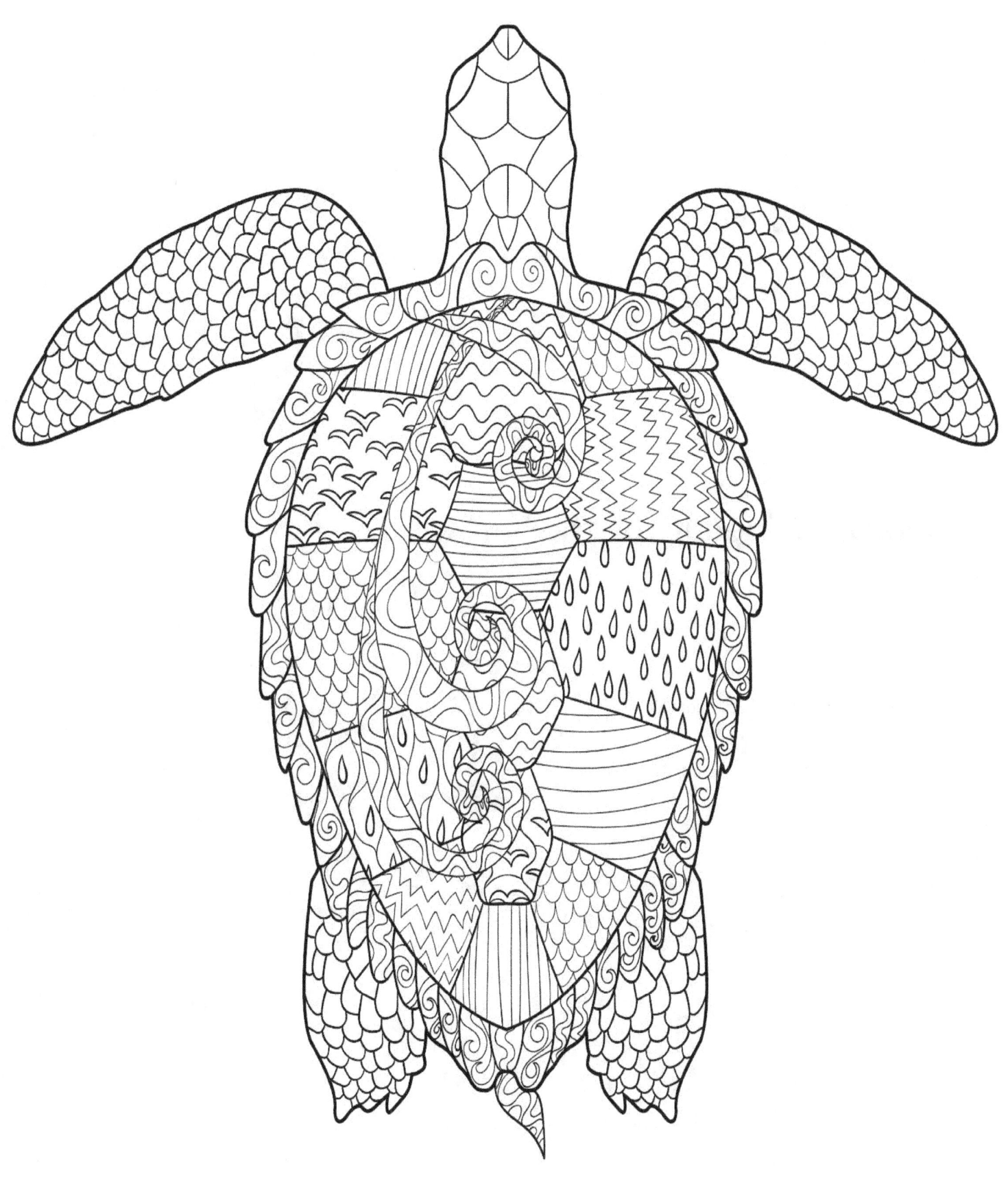

Toca: "Wipeout" by the Surfaris

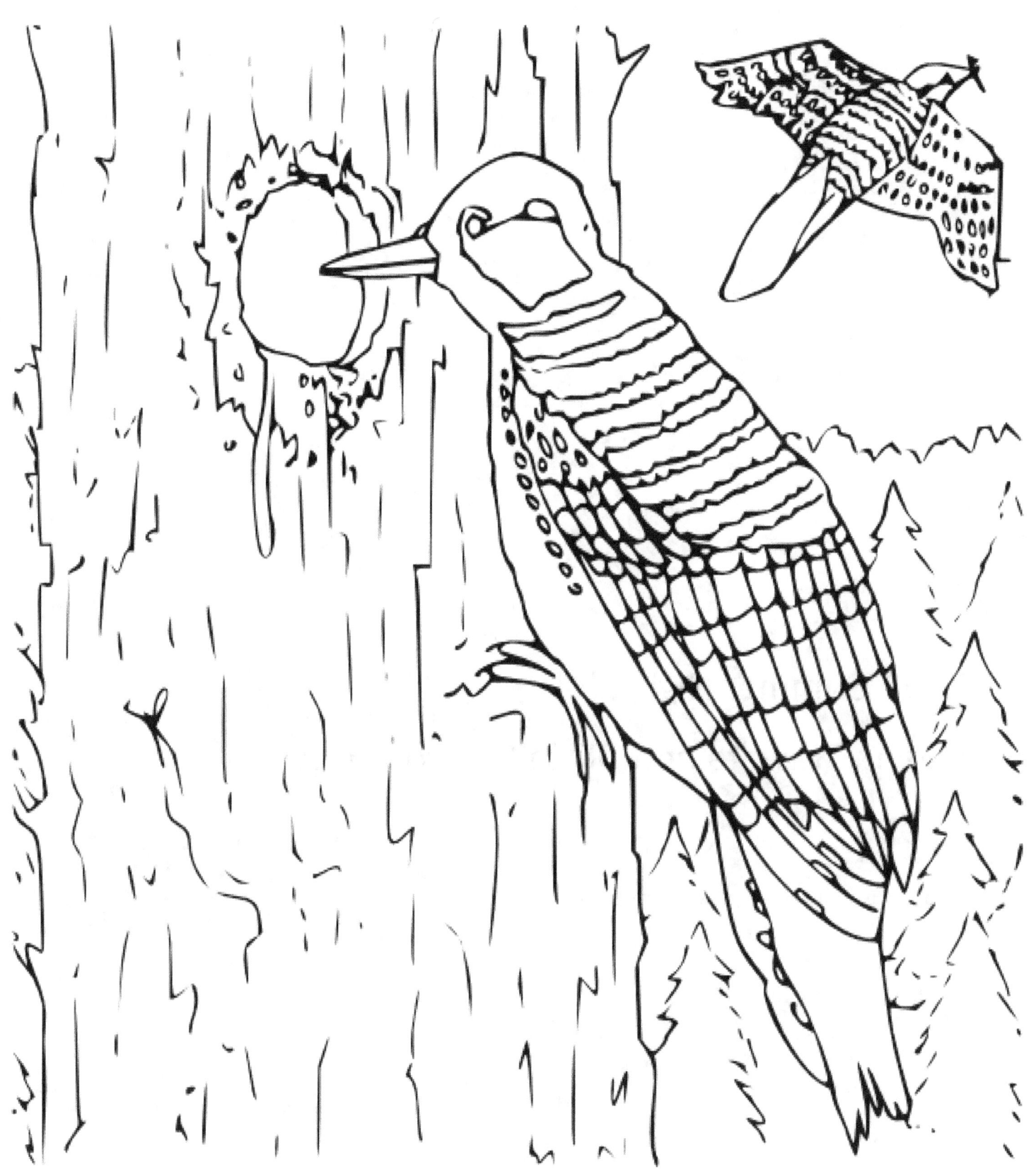

Toca: "Summer Nights"

by John Travolta and Olivia Newton-John

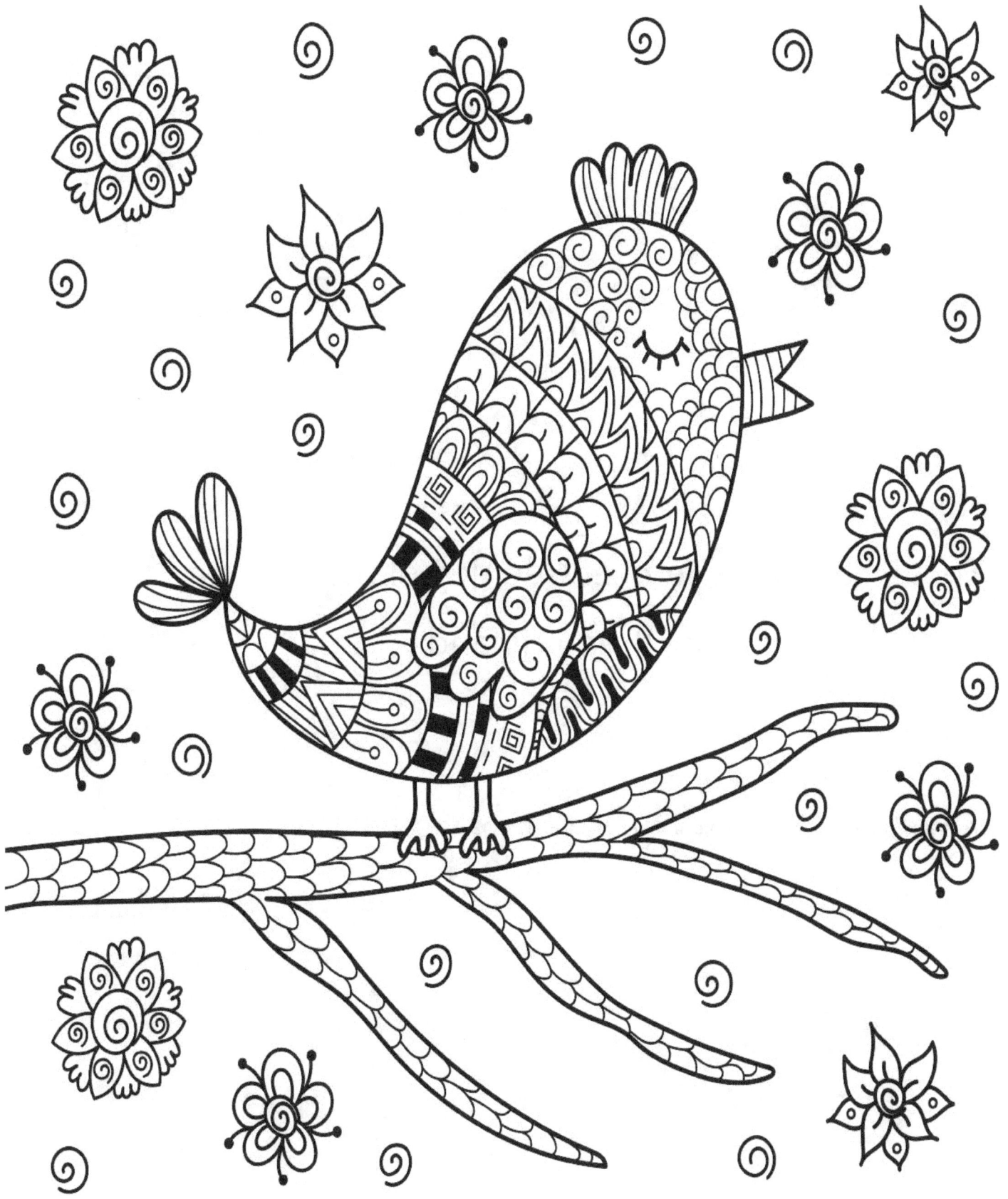

Toca: "Itsy Bitsy Teenie Weenie Yellow Polkadot Bikini" by Bryan Hyland

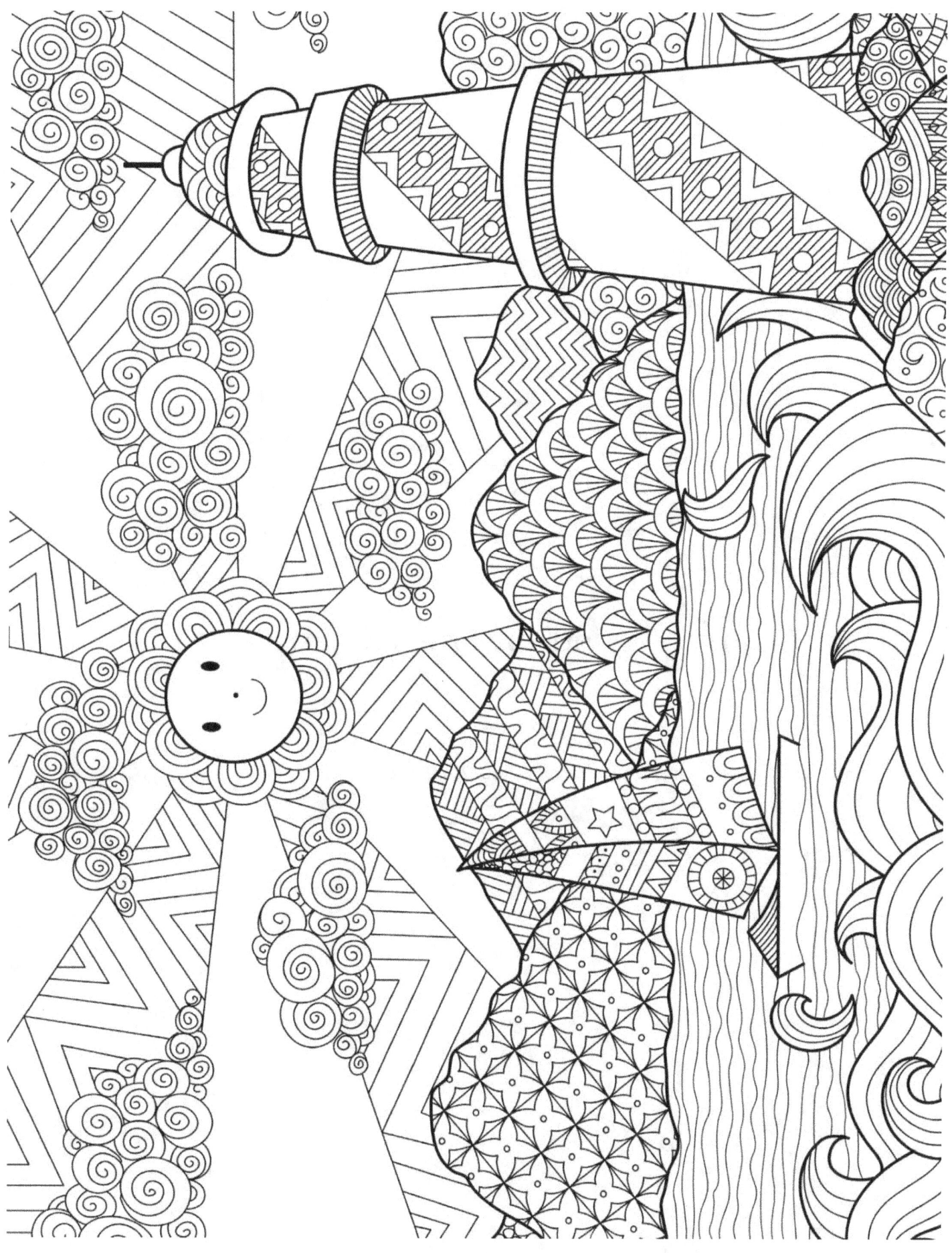

Toca: "Summer Wind" by Frank Sinatra

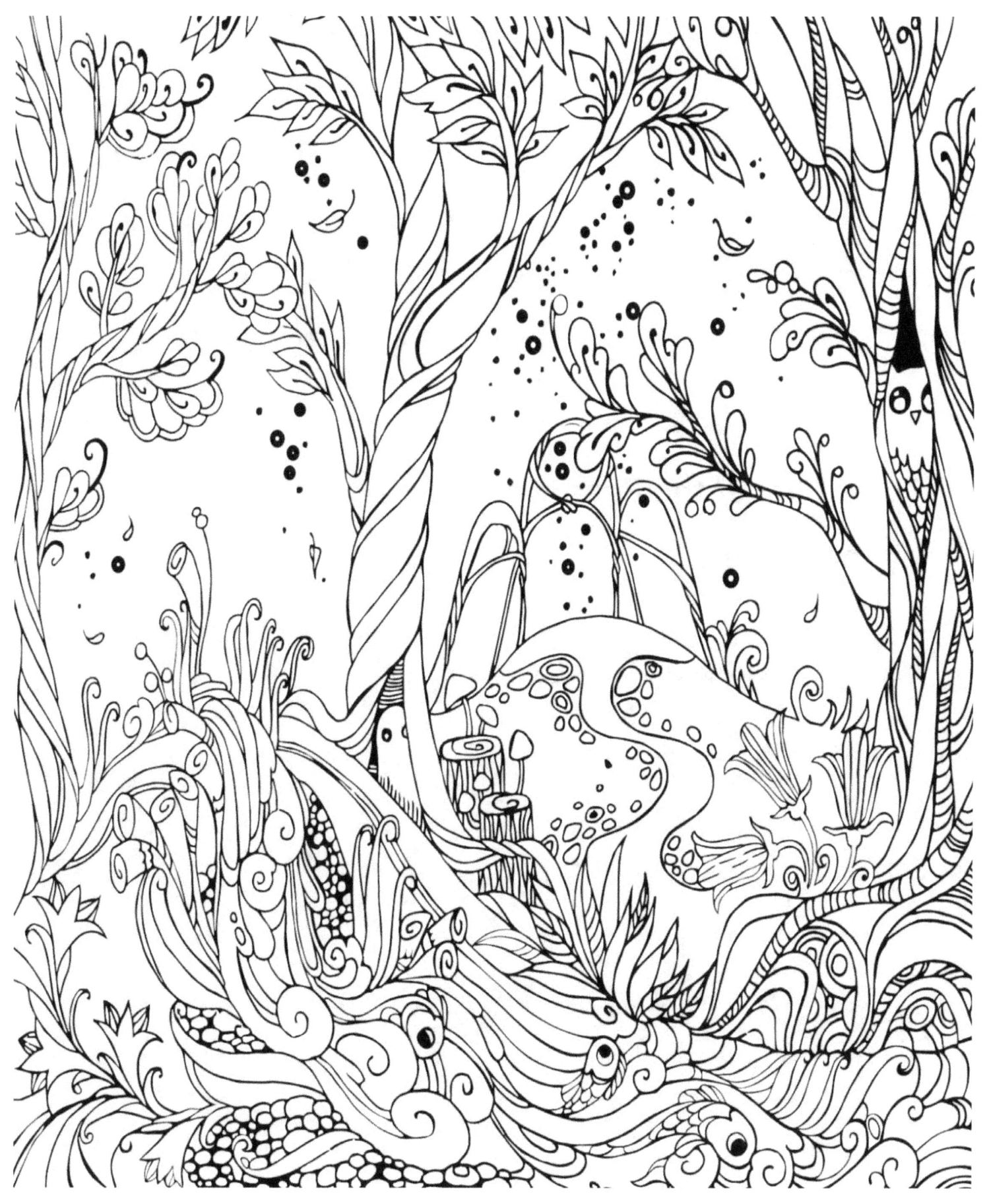

Toca: "Under the Boardwalk"

by the Drifters

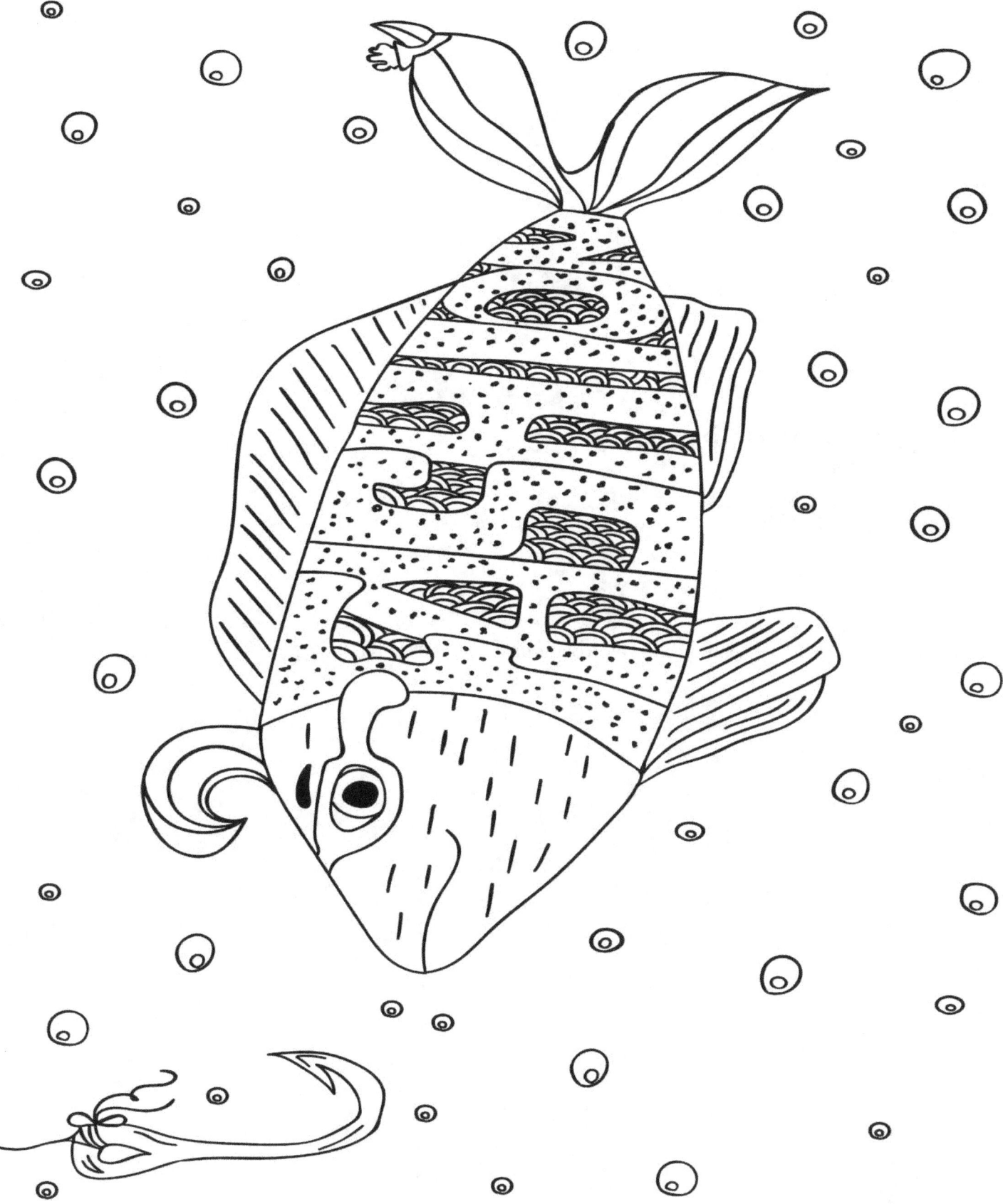

Toca: "Islands in the Stream"

by Kenny Rogers

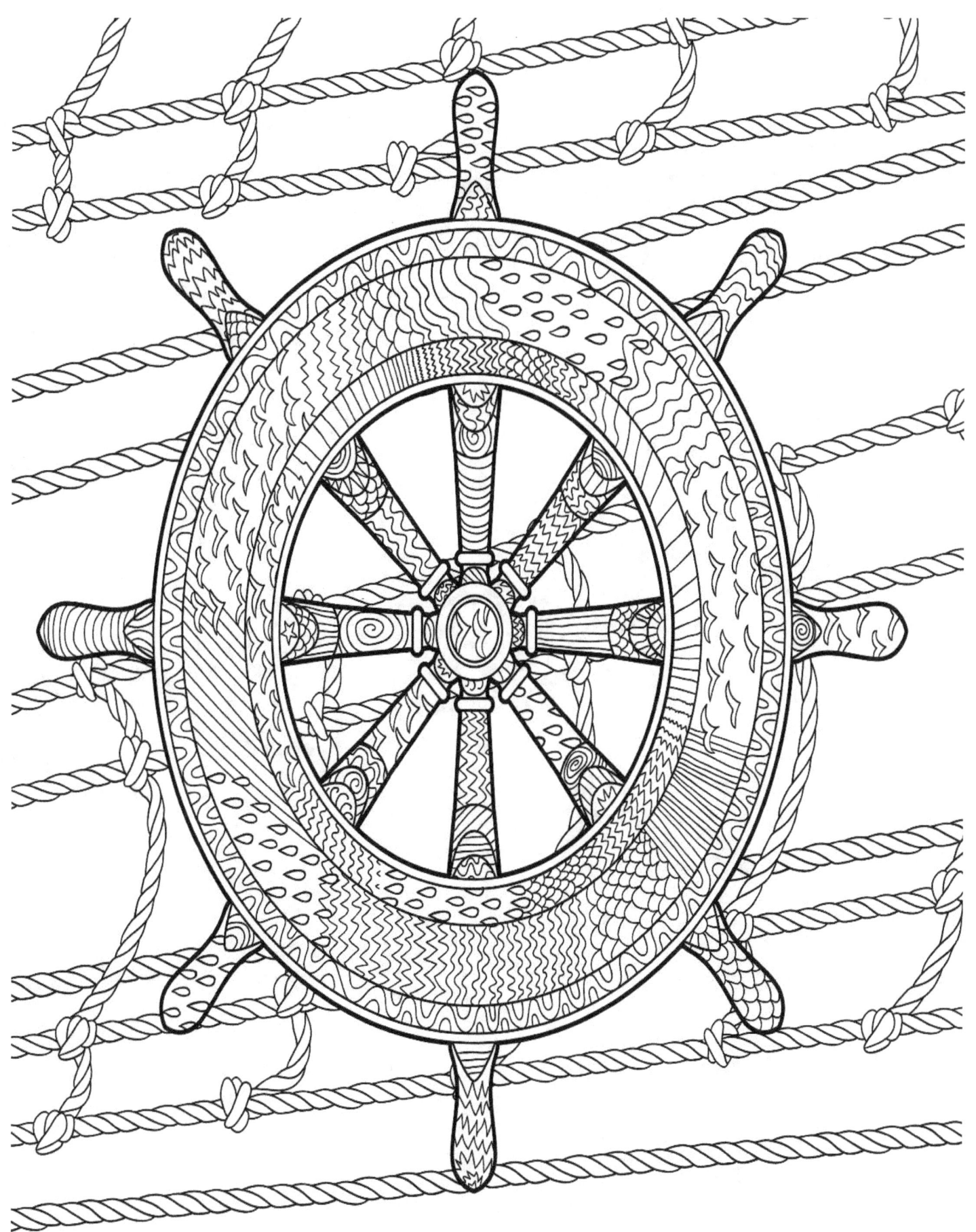